THE SECRET WIRELESS

Or, The Spy Hunt of the Camp Brady Patrol

I0616826

LEWIS E. THEISS

1st WORLD
LIBRARY
Literary Society

The Secret Wireless

Lewis E. Theiss

© 1st World Library, 2009
PO Box 2211
Fairfield, IA 52556
www.1stworldlibrary.com
First Edition

LCCN: 2009923473

Softcover ISBN: 978-1-4218-8861-3
Hardcover ISBN: 978-1-4218-8960-3
eBook ISBN: 978-1-4218-8762-3

Purchase *"The Secret Wireless"*
as a traditional bound book at:
www.1stWorldLibrary.com/purchase.asp?ISBN=978-1-4218-8861-3

1st World Library is a literary, educational organization
dedicated to:

- Creating a free internet library of downloadable ebooks

- Hosting writing competitions and offering book publishing
scholarships.

Interested in more 1st World Library books? contact:
literacy@1stworldlibrary.com
Check us out at: www.1stworldlibrary.com

1st World Library Literary Society

Giving Back to the World

"If you want to work on the core problem, it's early school literacy."

- James Barksdale, former CEO of Netscape

"No skill is more crucial to the future of a child, or to a democratic and prosperous society, than literacy."

- Los Angeles Times

"Literacy... means far more than learning how to read and write... The aim is to transmit... knowledge and promote social participation."

- UNESCO

"Literacy is not a luxury, it is a right and a responsibility. If our world is to meet the challenges of the twenty-first century we must harness the energy and creativity of all our citizens."

- President Bill Clinton

"Parents should be encouraged to read to their children, and teachers should be equipped with all available techniques for teaching literacy, so the varying needs and capacities of individual kids can be taken into account."

- Hugh Mackay

To

WALTER K. RHODES, A.M., E.E.,

PROFESSOR OF ELECTRO-TECHNICS
IN BUCKNELL UNIVERSITY,

TO WHOSE KINDLY HELPFULNESS IS DUE
WHATEVER OF TECHNICAL MERIT THERE MAY BE
IN THIS AND COMPANION STORIES OF THE
"WIRELESS,"

This Book is Dedicated

CONTENTS

CHAPTER I

WHAT CAME OF HENRY'S IDEA

Henry Harper was sitting in the doorway of the workshop in his father's back yard, where the Camp Brady Wireless Club made their headquarters. He was reading the morning newspaper. Suddenly he sprang to his feet. His face grew black. His free hand clenched.

"That's terrible!" he exclaimed. "Terrible!"

He walked across the shop, spread the newspaper on the bench and began to read aloud the big head-lines that had so aroused him.

LEAK IN NAVY DEPARTMENT

Germans Knew of Departure of Transport Fleet
First Contingent of Pershing's Men Attacked,
by Waiting   Submarines

"It's terrible, terrible!" repeated Henry. "Their spies are everywhere. They stop at nothing. Who could have been villain enough to give them the information? It is terrible!"

In his agitation Henry began to pace up and down the floor

of the shop. His face grew blacker and blacker as he brooded over the story of treachery. Though Henry was not yet eighteen, he was affected far more deeply by the story than most boys of his age would have been. For when the Camp Brady Wireless Club, of which Henry was president, had been practising the previous summer, Henry had been called upon to replace one of Uncle Sam's radio men who was suddenly stricken with appendicitis, and Henry had taken the operator's oath of fidelity to his government. So to him treachery appeared doubly black.

For some moments he paced up and down the shop. Suddenly he stopped short. A new idea had come to him.

"How did they get the news to Germany?" he asked aloud. "Both the cables and the mails are censored—and besides the mails would be too slow. It must have been the wireless. Can there be traitors in the wireless service, too?"

Henry was silent a moment, his brow wrinkled in thought. "Never!" he cried suddenly. "Uncle Sam's radio men are true blue. It's a secret wireless! A secret wireless! The Germans have got a hidden station somewhere."

The black look left his face. The scowl was replaced by a gleam of joy. "That means a job for us!" he cried. "The wireless patrol can help find that station, just as we found the German dynamiters at Elk City."

For when the wireless patrol had been at Camp Brady only a few weeks previously, acting as official operators for the commander of the troops guarding that section of the country, Roy Mercer had picked an innocent-looking message out of the air one night and by accident had found a code message in it revealing a German plot to dynamite a great dam and destroy a munition city; and later the wireless

Lewis E. Theiss

patrol had run down the dynamiters themselves in the very nick of time, after the state police had failed to find them, and had saved the city.

With Henry, to think was to act. "I'll write Captain Hardy at once," he said to himself.

Captain Hardy was a young physician who had been leader of the club of boys that had camped on his father's farm near old Fort Brady, and that had subsequently become the Camp Brady Wireless Club. But Captain Hardy was no longer leader of the club. He had offered his services to his country, and was now Captain Hardy of the Medical Officers' Reserve Corps. It was his standing and his friendship with the Chief of the Radio Service that had made it possible to secure permission for the Camp Brady boys to act as radio men for the state troops the preceding summer, although the government had forbidden amateurs to send wireless messages. And Henry, believing that his idolized leader could accomplish anything, now cleared a space at his desk in a corner of the shop, and wrote him a long letter, setting forth all that was in his heart.

The promptness with which the answer came should have warned Henry that the reply was not the one he hoped for. But his faith in his leader was so great that he never doubted for a moment that if Captain Hardy favored the proposal, he could effect its accomplishment. With a shout of joy, Henry seized the letter from the hand of the postman and ran to his favorite haunt, the workshop, to read it. As he did so, the smile faded from his face and a look of utter despair succeeded it, for this was what he read:

"MY DEAR HENRY:

"It was a very great pleasure to receive your letter, with

the little items of information about the members of the club, and your plan to be helpful in the present emergency. I know exactly how you feel. Every true American is filled with similar loathing for the treacherous enemies that infest our land, and with the same ardent desire to hunt them down and bring them to justice. You may be very sure that our secret service men are hard on the trail of many of them. Yet the very story of treachery that has so stirred your indignation shows that the secret service men cannot cope with them. But the fault is not with the secret service. It lies with Congress, which has persistently refused to appropriate sufficient money to make the service adequate. As far as it goes, it is the peer of any secret service. Of course help is needed, but I very much fear it is not the sort of assistance that the Camp Brady boys are prepared to give.

"You see, Henry, there are two possibilities. Either there is a leak in the navy department itself, as your story says, or else the sailing of the troops was observed at the port of embarkation and their destination guessed at. There is nothing you could do in the way of apprehending a spy in Washington, and I doubt if you could be of much assistance in detecting German agents in our ports. Of course I know how skilful the boys are with their wireless, especially you and Willie Brown, and I know what close observers Roy Mercer and Lew Heinsling are. And I realize, too, that in running down the dynamiters at the Elk City reservoir after both the Pennsylvania troops and the state police had failed, you proved that the wireless patrol was a mighty efficient organization. But that campaign was accomplished in the mountains and forests where your training in scouting and woodcraft has made you at home. Conditions in a great seaport would be so strange and confusing to all of you that I fear you would be more of a hindrance than a help.

"I am sorry about it, for I know how keenly you feel and how eager you are to help your country. The best way you can do that is to continue in school, learning all you can and making yourselves more and more efficient as wireless operators. In a very short time, I suspect, Uncle Sam will be in pressing need of good radio men. Then, although you are still young, your chance will come; for your ability is already known to the Chief of the Radio Service through your capture of the dynamiters last summer.

"As you know, our camp is just outside of Washington. I happen to be going into the city to-morrow. Of course, I shall take occasion to lay your suggestion before the Chief. But do not build any hopes on that statement. I have no idea anything will come of it. But it may help the Chief to bear you in mind later on. I am sorry to dash your hopes, but I cannot do otherwise than to tell you the truth. Of course if anything should come of it, I will let you know promptly. Remember me to all the other boys.

"Sincerely yours,

"JAMES HARDY."

Henry's face became longer and longer as he read. When he had finished the letter there was more than a suspicion of moisture in his eyes.

"Oh!" he cried, "if only I could be with Captain Hardy when he sees the Chief of the Radio Service, I'd *make* the Chief understand that we can help. We could be just as useful to the radio men as the Baker Street Irregulars were to Sherlock Holmes. Oh! I just wish I could be with him. I wonder when he will see the Chief."

Henry picked up the envelope and examined the postmark. "This was mailed yesterday morning," he muttered, "and Captain Hardy said he was going to Washington to-morrow. That's to-day. Maybe he's with him this afternoon. Maybe he went this morning. I'm sure he knows by this time what the result is. Oh! I wish I were with him. I'd just *make* that Radio Chief take us."

As he spoke a telegraph messenger entered the yard. He caught sight of Henry in the workshop door. "Hey!" he called. "Does Henry Harper live here? Got a message for him."

Henry was almost too much amazed to answer. He had never received a telegram in his life before.

"Hey!" called the messenger again. "Are you asleep?"

"No," was the answer, "and I'm Henry Harper."

"Then why didn't you say so?"

Henry ran forward and seized the yellow envelope. "Where's it from?" he asked.

"Washington," said the messenger.

"Washington!" repeated Henry. "Washington! Then we're to go."

"If you'll sign here," said the messenger, "I'll go. I can't stand here all day. Nothin' to pay."

Henry signed the messenger's book, then tore open the envelope and took out the following telegram: "Want you, Roy, Lew, and Willie to meet me Pennsylvania Station New York City Friday two P. M. for work suggested in your letter."

CHAPTER II

HENRY OVERCOMES AN OBSTACLE

Could the messenger boy have seen Henry after the latter had read the telegram, he would soon have changed his mind as to Henry's sleepiness. For a very brief space—just long enough to reread the message once or twice—Henry stood like one dazed, as motionless as a statue, and as silent as a sign-post. Then he gave a loud whoop and began to dance around the little shop. For a boy who was ordinarily so sober as Henry, such conduct was scandalously riotous. He skipped about the tiny wireless room, waving his hat in his hand, cheering for the Camp Brady Wireless Patrol, and making loud declarations as to what that organization would do to the enemies of the country.

Ordinarily Henry would have restrained himself. Not even the news that the Camp Brady Patrol had been selected to perform the wireless service at the guard headquarters the preceding summer had excited Henry as did this message from his captain. But that was scarcely to be wondered at. The work for the commander of the Pennsylvania guards had promised nothing but the sending of uninteresting and wordy despatches, though to be sure it had turned out quite differently before it was ended. But the task now in view promised excitement from the start. It breathed adventure, romance. To hunt spies—to trace traitors—to turn the searchlight on hidden crimes and dark deeds—to outwit clever men—to take a man's part in a man's world—to do deeds of daring and bravery—and above all to serve his country and save his fellows—these were the things that came into his mind as the probable results of the precious communication he held in his hand.

Forgotten were the tedious hours of monotony that his sober senses would have told him must make up the greater part of any such labor as that he was now about to embark upon. Forgotten were the dull, deadly dull and uninteresting days that his experience should have told him lay before him. In his enthusiasm Henry saw only the bright spots. The mental vision he looked upon glowed with rosy light. And Henry gave himself up utterly to enjoyment of the prospect.

So he danced and shouted and waved his hat, and cheered for the Camp Brady Patrol, until in his excitement he danced too close to the side of the tiny shop. His wildly waving hat came into contact with sundry tools and kettles and other metal implements hung up on nails to be out of the way. Down came saws and pails and a sprinkling can, and the hoe, and a dozen other articles in a noisy crash. It sounded as though a cyclone had suddenly descended upon the little shop, or a 42-centimeter shell had burst within. The exultant chant of the lone occupant of the building suddenly ceased. But its place was instantly taken by another voice as Henry's mother suddenly appeared on the back porch of the house, looking anxiously toward the workshop.

"Henry! Henry!" came her anxious call.

"Yes, mother," replied Henry, disentangling himself from the wreckage, and thrusting his head out of the shop door. "What is it?"

"Whatever are you doing?" demanded Mrs. Harper. "I thought the shop had tumbled in."

"It's only some things I knocked down," laughed Henry. Then his enthusiasm bubbled over again. "Just think, mother," he cried. "We're going! We're going! Captain Hardy has sent for us!"

Mrs. Harper looked at her son anxiously. His words meant absolutely nothing to her, for Henry had not told any one of his letter to his captain. Suddenly she feared that perhaps something had fallen on Henry's head and momentarily unbalanced him.

"Going?" she said. "Where? What are you talking about?"

"We're going to New York City to help catch German spies," cried Henry, beginning to dance about again in his excitement. "Isn't it bully! And we'll catch 'em, too, just as we did the dynamiters."

"I guess you're going crazy," said his mother. Then as Henry continued his demonstration, his mother said sharply, "You stop right there, Henry Harper, and tell me what all this nonsense means about German spies and New York and Captain Hardy. You know very well that Captain Hardy is in Washington with the army."

Henry at once calmed down and took a grip on himself. "Yes, mother," he said. "Captain Hardy was in Washington, but he is going to New York—"

"How do you know?" interrupted Mrs. Harper impatiently.

"He just telegraphed me—"

"Telegraphed you!" said the incredulous Mrs. Harper. "What would Captain Hardy be telegraphing to a youngster like you for, I'd like to know."

"In answer to my letter—" began Henry, but again his mother cut him short.

"Your letter?" she said. "What letter? I didn't know that you had written him a letter."

"You see, mother," said Henry patiently, "when I read in the newspapers the other day that the Germans had found out about the sailing of Pershing's men, and had sent submarines to lay in wait for them out in the ocean, the idea came to me that perhaps the wireless patrol could help to discover—"

"Henry Harper, I hope you never had the impudence to suggest that you youngsters could—"

"I did, mother. But I don't think it was impudence. I wrote to Dr. Hardy and asked if the wireless patrol couldn't help catch the spies who are sending news to Germany."

"Well of all things!" ejaculated Mrs. Harper. "What will you infants do next? Offer to relieve the President of his job?"

"Well, we did catch the dynamiters at the Elk City reservoir," protested Henry defensively. "And we did it after the state police and the national guards had failed. I don't see why we can't help catch German spies in New York just as well as in Pennsylvania."

"Humph!" said Mrs. Harper. "It's a lot of help you young-sters would be in catching real spies. You just happened to stumble on these dynamiters and now you think you can do thing. But that's the way with boys. They're all alike."

"But, mother," protested Henry, "boys can be useful in lots of ways. And just because they are boys nobody thinks of suspecting them."

"There's one place where a certain boy I know could be of a lot of use and never be suspected," agreed Mrs. Harper. "And that's at that woodpile back of the shed."

"Please don't interrupt me, mother," said Henry. "You asked me to tell you about our trip to New York."

"About your dream of a trip to New York," corrected Mrs. Harper. "You don't for one minute think you are really going to New York, do you?"

"Indeed we are," replied Henry. "And this is how it came about. When I read of the leak in the navy's secrets and the attempts of the Germans to torpedo our transports, I wrote to Captain Hardy about it. I told him we could be just as useful catching German spies in New York as we were in Pennsylvania. He answered and said he didn't think we could be of any use, but—"

"Showed his sense," interrupted Mrs. Harper.

"But he said," continued Henry, paying no attention to the interruption, "that he would mention the matter to the Chief of the Radio Service and let me know if anything came of it. And something has come of it, mother. Just think! We're to go. Here's the telegram itself."

Mrs. Harper took the yellow paper that Henry held out to her and read it slowly and carefully. "Well, I never!" she said at last. "I never did! But I don't know whether to let you go or not. Why, you'd be lost inside of ten minutes in New York, and instead of being a help to the police, you'd keep them busy hunting for you. I don't know about this. Wait till your father gets home and we'll talk it over."

"But, mother," protested Henry, "I can't wait. And we've *got* to go. The Chief of the Radio Service has asked for our help. That means the government wants us. If it wants us, it must need us. And we've just got to go."

"Humph!" said Mrs. Harper.

"And besides," added Henry, reading the signs in his mother's face, "Dr. Hardy is to be in New York with us, so we can't get into trouble."

"Well, that alters the case," said Mrs. Harper. "With Dr. Hardy to look after you, I reckon you *can't* go very far astray."

"Then we can go, mother?"

"I suppose so. I know your father thinks every one of us should do everything he possibly can to help win this war. But it gets me to know what you youngsters can do that will be of any use. Still, I guess the government wouldn't have sent for you if it didn't want you, and I won't stand in the road of the government."

"Hurrah!" shouted Henry. "Then I'm off to tell the others." And he darted out of the yard and was away like an arrow.

Lewis E. Theiss

CHAPTER III

THE WIRELESS PATROL PREPARES FOR ACTION

At top speed Henry tore down the street.

Half a block from his home he passed a schoolmate.

"Hey! What's your hurry?" the latter called out, as Henry dashed past him.

"Wireless patrol ordered out!" Henry shouted over his shoulder, as he darted on down the street.

"Wait a minute!" called the other lad.

"Can't," cried Henry. "Got to get the patrol together to go on a spy hunt."

At the words "spy hunt" the other boy leaped forward and ran after Henry at top speed. "What's up?" he asked enviously, as he overtook Henry and raced along beside him. For the lad did not belong to the wireless patrol.

"Ordered to New York by the government," panted Henry, "to hunt for German spies."

The announcement had all the effect Henry intended it to have. For a full half minute his companion said never a word, but ran mutely beside him, his eyes fastened incredulously on Henry. Then, "Gee whiz!" he said. "You're not really goin' to New York!"

"Sure thing," panted Henry. "Just got a telegram from Washington."

That was too much for Henry's companion. "Gee whiz!" he said again. "I wish I belonged to the wireless patrol."

Henry looked at him sympathetically, half sorry that he had said what he had. "Maybe you will some day," he replied. "Good-bye."

They had reached the home of wee Willie Brown. Henry stopped abruptly and turned in at the open gate. He mounted the steps and rang the bell. Mrs. Brown opened the door.

"Is Willie—at home—Mrs. Brown?" he asked, all out of breath.

"Yes, Henry," replied Mrs. Brown. "You'll find him up in his room."

"Is he busy?"

"Oh! He's tinkering with his wireless, as usual," said Mrs. Brown. "But he's always glad to see you, Henry."

"He will be this time, I'm sure," said Henry. "The wireless patrol is ordered out on a spy hunt."

"What! Not again?" queried Mrs. Brown, in astonishment. "Where are you going this time?"

"To New York," rejoined Henry, and his voice plainly showed his exultation.

"Tell me more about it." Mrs. Brown was at once all seriousness.

Henry turned away from the stair door and explained the situation to Mrs. Brown, who was very sober. But when Henry said that Dr. Hardy had asked the boys to come and that he would himself be with them in New York, the serious look vanished from Mrs. Brown's face. "That's all right, then," she said. "If Dr. Hardy wants you and is to be there to look after you, it is all right. I am glad Willie has the opportunity to go. He has never been in a really big city."

Henry went on up to Willie's room and broke the news to him. And the sounds that came down to Mrs. Brown made her laugh heartily. But it was a laugh of sympathy. She remembered that she had once been young herself. Presently the racket up-stairs subsided. Then came the clatter of noisy and eager feet on the stairs. And a moment later Henry and Willie skipped out of the door, tore through the gate, and went racing up the street toward Roy Mercer's house.

But Roy was not at home. He was, as Henry had suspected he would be, at work in the garage where he had been employed during the school vacation. But Henry thought it would be well to secure permission from Mrs. Mercer for Roy to take the trip to New York, for she was inclined to be rather strict with Roy.

"Captain Hardy has just sent me a request for four of the boys of the wireless patrol to come to New York," said Henry, diplomatically, "and Roy is one of the four he wants. We came to see if he may go."

Mrs. Mercer looked at Henry keenly. "What are you going to do in New York," she demanded, "and who's to pay the bills?"

"I don't know exactly what we're to do," said Henry, "but we're to help the wireless service. I think they want us to listen in and pick up low-length messages that the high-powered government stations don't get. The government will pay our expenses."

"Humph!" said Mrs. Mercer. Then she was silent a moment in thought. "When does Dr. Hardy want you to go?"

"He wants us to meet him in New York at two o'clock Friday afternoon. That means we should have to leave here on the early morning train Friday."

"I don't know about this," said Mrs. Mercer. "All play and no work is just as bad for a boy as no play and all work. And Roy has done nothing but play all summer. He has been at that camp of yours ever since school closed. And besides, he is earning three dollars a week working at the garage."

Henry had feared that Mrs. Mercer would object to Roy's going. Roy's father had been sick and unable to work for some weeks, and Henry knew that the three dollars Roy earned each week were badly needed in the Mercer home.

"I think that the government will pay Roy more than he earns now," explained Henry. "And I hope that you will let him go because Captain Hardy wants only certain boys and Roy is one of them. He is very necessary to the success of our work."

"I'll see what Roy's father says," was the reply, and Mrs. Mercer vanished within the house.

Meantime Henry and Willie stood on the porch hardly daring to speak to one another, so fearful were they that Roy might not be allowed to go. When Mrs. Mercer suddenly appeared again and announced briefly that Roy could go, they thanked her, and as soon as they could get around a corner, they gave vent to their feelings in a loud whoop.

Lew Heinsling was picked up a few minutes later, with no objection on the part of his parents, and the three boys raced to the garage, where they imparted the news to Roy.

School, which normally should already have been in session, had been kept from opening by an epidemic of measles; and no one knew when it would convene. But there was no apparent chance of an early opening, for the epidemic was then at its worst. There was no obstacle now in the way of the four boys. Roy got his employer's permission to leave the garage for an hour, and the four boys hurried to the wireless patrol headquarters in Henry's shop, to discuss the adventure that lay before them.

That night the entire patrol assembled in the little workshop and those who were not to go enviously discussed the coming adventure with the four who had been summoned to duty. For no one in the patrol doubted that the expedition would end in adventure and excitement, to say nothing of the delights of a trip to the nation's metropolis. Their common experience in running down the dynamiters at the Elk City reservoir gave these boys the certainty that both adventure and danger lay ahead of their four lucky fellows. But could they have known how truly thrilling and adventurous were the days ahead of their companions; could they have foreseen all the strange and exciting situations that would confront their fellows; could they have guessed the part their comrades of the wireless patrol were about to play in wiping out this hidden menace to our troops on the ocean, they would have been envious indeed.

But they could not know these things. And they recognized the fact that Captain Hardy had asked for these four because of their superior attainments, because they were best fitted to do the work in hand. So the stay-at-homes loyally crushed down their feeling of envy and united in a hearty send-off for their fellows. Every member of the patrol was at the railroad station Friday morning to bid good-bye to their four comrades who were to play no inconspicuous part in the stirring days to come, and who were to make known to the country at large the name of the Camp Brady Wireless Patrol.

Lewis E. Theiss

CHAPTER IV

THE SCENE OF ACTION

As the conductor shouted "All aboard!" the little group of boys on the station platform suddenly parted, and the four who had stood in the centre of the ring, vigorously shaking hands, now moved hastily toward the train and scrambled up the steps. The conductor waved his signal to the engine-driver and swung aboard. The locomotive bell began to ring, there was a hissing of steam, and a puffing of the great locomotive, and the train slid gently forward. On the car platform stood the four departing members of the wireless patrol, waving fond farewells to their less fortunate members. Then they turned and entered the coach, with the cheers of their comrades ringing in their ears, their hearts beating with high determination to give all that they had of strength and skill and courage and patience to the grim task that lay ahead of them.

In no time Central City was lost from sight. The familiar fields and woods vanished. The country grew strange. Soon they were passing through a region entirely unknown to them. But so busy was each boy with his thoughts that he hardly noticed what at other times would have held his closest attention; for the pictures in each mind were just as unfamiliar as the landscape through which they were speeding.

"What was to be the nature of their work?" each boy was asking himself. "Would they sit and listen in, as they had done at Camp Brady, or would they be set to roving about, trying to pick out suspicious characters, or detect suspicious acts? And what would New York be like? What was there about this great, roaring city of men that was so attractive, that drew such multitudes to it, that grew with such uncanny swiftness? What was New York like, anyway?"

And almost before they knew it, the train rolled into a tunnel, dived under a great river, and emerged again in a huge yard far below the level of the streets, that was filled with many tracks and closed in with enormous walls of cement. Then the train ran into a great shed and came to rest. The boys left the coach, mounted a long flight of iron steps and found themselves in the city of their dreams—New York.

And there, at the gateway, was their beloved captain. They swarmed about him and grasped his hand. Then Captain Hardy led them to a corner of the waiting-room that offered a little privacy, and there they sat down in a group, close to one another, to talk over the business that had brought them again together.

"As I wrote you in my letter, Henry," said Captain Hardy, "I was not at all hopeful that your plan would meet with official encouragement. But I had promised you that I would mention it to the Chief of the Radio Service and I did so. It didn't take him a minute to decide on it. To my surprise he said he wanted you. 'I haven't a bit of doubt,' said he, 'that the country's full of secret German wireless outfits. They are probably of small sending power and operate in unusual wave lengths. It is almost impossible for our regular service to detect them. In fact I don't know how we are ever going to locate them unless we organize the amateurs all over the country so that they can listen in and catch practically everything that goes through the air. We are not able to do that yet, but I shall be very glad to have the help of your boys. I've been mighty interested in the way they handled that affair at Elk City. They are experienced and have good sense. They should be very useful to Uncle Sam.'" Dr. Hardy paused and smiled. "You see," he went on, "the Chief has kept pretty close watch of you boys. He knows all about the affair at Elk City." And Captain Hardy smiled affectionately at his charges.

"What are the Radio Chief's instructions?" asked Roy. "What are we to do?"

"The Radio Service," replied Captain Hardy, "has no agencies for making arrests and detecting crime. So we shall work under the direction of the secret service and in cooperation with the police. And our first duty is to make ourselves known to both."

"If the Chief of the Radio Service wanted the wireless patrol," said Roy, "why did you telegraph for just the four of us? And why are we in New York instead of Washington?"

"You couldn't be of any use in Washington," said Captain Hardy, "but you may be of a great deal of service here. You see New York is a difficult place to guard. This is our principal port. It is so vast that it is next to impossible to watch all of it, and there are hundreds of thousands of Germans or people of German descent living here. The Radio Chief needs sharp eyes and ears as well as trained fingers just now, and he knows that you boys combine these qualifications. He suggested that I send for four of you and see what you could accomplish. I chose you four because you have shown the greatest ability along the lines necessary."

A flush of pleasure glowed in each of the faces before him.

For a moment Willie Brown forgot where he was, forgot the crowd and the great station and the strange sights and sounds about him, forgot even why he was in New York, while his mind went back to that first summer at Camp Brady, when he had been the most backward, self-distrustful, helpless lad in camp. Now he was chosen to serve his government, to do work of the greatest importance for his country; and he had been selected because of his ability. No wonder Willie blessed the day he first saw Camp Brady. No wonder his eyes were wet with a grateful mist as he looked affectionately at his captain, who had made him what he was.

But Willie had little time for revery. Roy was speaking again, asking another of those sharp questions that showed very well why he should have been chosen as a spy hunter, or for anything else that required keenness of mind.

"What about yourself?" Roy was saying. "Do you have to go back to your medical duties? We can work ever so much better with you to lead us than we could with a stranger."

Roy alone had grasped the possibility that Captain Hardy might not be able to remain with them. Now every eye was fixed anxiously on Captain Hardy's face.

"No," he said, "I do not have to return to Washington. It is of the utmost importance to catch these spies and the government could well afford to give up one ordinary doctor in order to get four skilled spy hunters." He paused and smiled, then added: "So I have been detailed to special duty in New York."

The boys could hardly repress a shout of joy.

"And my instructions," continued Captain Hardy, "were to get into touch with the police and the secret service immediately. As I have told you, we must get acquainted with both. But before we do, I suggest that we take a look at the town where we are to work in the days to come. Let's be moving."

They rose and passed through the station. Its great vaulted ceiling, half as high as a church steeple, its huge flights of steps, its enormous corridors, its wonderful stonework, dwarfing into insignificance anything they had ever seen before, fairly awed the boys from Central City. It was Roy's keen eye that caught sight of the great maps of the world high up on the walls. The crowds of people coming and going hardly seemed like crowds, so vast was the structure. With reluctant feet the four boys pushed on. But when they had mounted the steps to the arcade and caught sight of the illuminated transparencies showing scenes along the railway's path, they came to a dead stop. For Willie Brown, with his almost uncanny eye for landscapes, at once declared that a certain picture represented a mountain scene not twenty-five miles from Central City; and when the others appealed to Captain Hardy, the latter confirmed Willie's statement.

When the four lads reached the sidewalk they were almost distracted. Thousands of people were hurrying along, passing in endless throngs up and down the street. Never had the boys from Central City seen people in such a rush.

"What's the hurry?" demanded Roy. "Why does everybody walk so fast? What's up?"

"Nothing," replied Captain Hardy, with a smile. "That's just the New York gait. Everybody walks fast here, and does everything else fast; and if you boys want to make a reputation in New York you'll have to hustle some. But I don't want you to make that kind of a reputation," he continued, hastily yanking Willie Brown from in front of a passing motor-car. "You will have to keep your eyes open here."

And indeed they had to. Motor-cars were rushing about as numerous as flies in August. Trolley-cars followed one another up and down Seventh Avenue in endless process-sions. Wagons and trucks stretched along the highway in slow-moving lines as far as the eye could see. Bells were ringing, whistles tooting, horns blowing, motor-cars honking, newsies shouting. The grinding of car-wheels, the rattle of carts, the clatter of hoofs on the asphalt, the shuffling of feet on the sidewalk, and a thousand other noises combined to make an indescribable and confusing roar. The noise and bustle were bewildering.

"I guess mother was right," thought Henry. "It would be mighty easy to get lost here. The wireless patrol will have to look sharp or the police will be called upon to find it."

And indeed there were so many distracting things that the four spy hunters found it difficult not to get lost. At every step something new and unfamiliar claimed their attention and caused them to pause and look about.

Captain Hardy let his charges go at their own gait. He paused when they wanted to look at something, took sharp care of them at crossings, and told them how to cross the streets so as to avoid accidents. And ever he kept his eye on them to see that none of the four became separated from the group. It pleased him to note how quickly they learned to avoid the traffic and dodge difficulties. Their training in observation had not been in vain.

To Herald Square the captain led his party. There, in a little eddy of sidewalk traffic, he drew them together.

"The streets that run lengthwise of the island," he said, "are called avenues, and the one before you is Sixth Avenue. The station we just left faces on Seventh Avenue. The cross streets are numbered, and the one we are on is Thirty-fourth Street. Broadway comes up the island on a long diagonal. Right here where Broadway, Thirty-fourth Street, and Sixth Avenue intersect, is one of the busiest corners in the city. Overhead are two elevated railway tracks. On the ground are six street-car tracks, crossing one another. Under the surface are two subway tracks. So you have three layers of people passing and repassing above or below one another. I want you to remember what I have said as to the arrangement of the thoroughfares—avenues run north and south, streets east and west. If you get that thought in your mind, you won't go very far out of your way.

"And there is one thing more to remember. In some cities, such as Philadelphia, the street numbers run 100 to each block. Here the houses are numbered consecutively, and you can't tell by a number where a house is. But if you should need to know, go to the nearest drug store. Every New York drug store has a city directory. And in the back of the directory you will find a table that will show you approximately where to find the street number you want. Don't forget. If you are to do effective work, you must become so familiar with New York that you can find your way around as readily as you can in Central City. Sometimes it may be necessary for you to go from place to place in the shortest possible time and you must know not only how to get there, but also how to take advantage of short cuts. We'll get some maps after a time and study them."

His young companions plied their leader with a thousand questions. They wanted to know the names of all the big buildings in sight. They had all heard of the Waldorf-Astoria Hotel and they gazed up Thirty-fourth Street at this well-known hostelry with much curiosity. They had heard of the Times Building and were eager to see it.

"We can't spend much time sightseeing just now," said Captain Hardy. "We must get into touch with the police and the secret service people and get our instructions. Then we will take a day or two, if possible, and see something of the town. It is most important for you to become well acquainted with it at once. But I guess we can take time to slip up to Times Square. It's only eight blocks up Broadway. Now I want you boys to see everything you can as we go along, and to try to remember all that you see. Wherever you go you must remember that you are in New York to detect German spies and presumably to run down German wireless outfits. We don't know where they are. We may be looking at one this very instant. So keep your eyes open. If you see anything that resembles a wireless outfit, or that might be used for sending messages, take careful note of it. And keep your ears open for suspicious conversations. Because you are boys, people will be less careful in their talk when you are present than they would be with older people about. The more youthful and unsophisticated you can make yourselves appear, the better it will be for your purpose."

Slowly the little party made its way up Broadway. By degrees the lads became accustomed to the roar of the traffic and the rush of pedestrians. At Times Square they paused for a look at the great newspaper building that gives the place its name, and at the great hotels rising on every side. Then they passed down a long flight of steps and found themselves in a low, vaulted, underground subway station.

"Makes you think of the dugouts on the firing-line in France," suggested the quick-witted Roy.

An instant later a train thundered up to the platform and the boys boarded it. A short ride and a short walk took them to Police Headquarters.

Captain Hardy sent his card to the Police Commissioner, with the request for a brief interview. A few moments later he had presented his credentials and introduced his companions, and four delighted boys found themselves blushingly shaking hands with New York's famous chief of police, Arthur Woods. Briefly Captain Hardy stated the purpose of his visit and related the story of the capture of the Elk City dynamiters.

"I recall the incident distinctly," said the Commissioner. "The newspapers were full of it. And I recall that when I read the story I wished I had as accomplished and clever a squad of boys to help me with some of my hard problems."

The four boys flushed with happiness. But they were too much embarrassed to make any reply.

"Captain Hardy," said the Commissioner, "what is your plan of action?"

"We have none as yet. We are to work under the direction of the secret service. But we have not seen Chief Flynn yet. The boys just arrived."

"Let me make one suggestion to you," said the Commissioner, turning again to the boys. "Before you attempt to do any detective work make yourselves familiar with the city. Get some maps and study them until you know every street and alley. Take your maps and go over the city on foot. Put several days in at it. Become acquainted with the water-front, the piers, the surface cars, the subways, the ferries. Learn the city so that you can get around rapidly. Make the acquaintance of as many policemen, wireless operators, secret service men, and other persons as you can. Don't forget that a kind deed or a thoughtful act will help you to make friendships quicker than anything else; and make all the friends you can. In police work you never know who will be of assistance to you. And above all things don't talk. Don't tell a living soul about your purpose or your plans. Let Captain Hardy do that if it is necessary. Secrecy is absolutely essential to the success of your work. Unless you can get along without betraying yourselves you may as well go right back home. Remember the spies you are after are also after you. If they learn what you are, they might even take your lives."

"Commissioner Woods," said Captain Hardy, after a pause, "I have been wondering whether or not these boys should have some kind of passes that will enable them to get through the police lines. There may come times when it is of the highest importance that nothing shall interfere with them. What do you think about it?"

The Commissioner considered for a moment. "If I were sure they could be trusted with—"

"They can," interrupted Captain Hardy. "Absolutely."

"Very well then."

The Commissioner pressed a button on his desk. A clerk entered the room.

"Make out special police cards for Captain Hardy and these four lads," he said, naming the boys.

Again he turned to the young spy hunters. "The cards you are about to get," he said, "will pass you by any policeman or put you through any police line. Do not let any one know you have them and never use them unless you absolutely must. It is best that not even the police should know who you are. Be very careful not to lose your cards."

"We will make some little cloth bags," said Henry, "and carry the cards in them inside of our underclothes."

"I see that you are resourceful," smiled the Commissioner.

The clerk returned with the cards and handed them to Captain Hardy.

"Before you go," said the Commissioner, "perhaps you would like to see our wireless department and get acquainted with Sergeant Pearce who is in charge of it."

He summoned a patrolman to guide them to the wireless rooms and wished the boys success.

A few moments later Sergeant Pearce was showing them the apparatus. Two operators sat at a wonderful Marconi outfit with receivers clamped to their ears. In another room various instruments were installed here and there, the walls were covered with diagrams of wireless instruments and outfits, and lines of men were sitting at long tables with receivers at their ears. It was the police wireless school. High above the roof the aerial hung, suspended between the main dome and a smaller dome at one end of the building.

"We are going to equip every station-house with wireless," said Sergeant Pearce, "and the men you saw at work in the school are being trained for operators. We have put wireless outfits on some of the patrol-wagons and on the police boat *Patrol*, so you see we can get into touch instantly with any precinct or with the *Patrol* no matter in what part of the harbor she may be. And when you have as big a harbor as we have, with several hundred miles of waterfront, that means something."

From Police Headquarters the little party went directly to the Post Office Building, near the Brooklyn Bridge, to see Chief Flynn. He was a large, heavy man, with black hair and eyes and a short mustache. He shook hands with each of the party, and gave each a searching look. He spoke quietly but right to the point.

"I had word from Washington about you," he said. "Do you know anything about the city?"

The boys admitted their ignorance.

"Then your first job is to get acquainted with New York. Get some maps and guide-books. While you are getting your bearings you can establish a wireless watch. I have a number of outfits in different parts of the city. For the next week or two, while you are getting acquainted with the city, I want you to maintain a twenty-four-hour watch at a place I shall send you to. Divide the time among you so that some one is listening in all the time. Here are the call signals of all the legitimate plants you will hear, either on land or water. Pay particular attention to call signals. If you catch one not in this list, be sure to get every word sent and let me hear from you at once. We have other operators listening in for messages of the usual commercial wave lengths and for very long wave lengths, so you need watch only for messages of less than three hundred meters."

He wrote an address on a slip of paper and gave it to Captain Hardy. "Go there," he directed. "A wireless outfit has been installed and accommodations await you."

He took the slip of paper from Captain Hardy and wrote

Lewis E. Theiss

some figures on it. "That," said he, "is my private telephone number. But do not bother me unless you get hold of something important."

In another moment the wireless party found itself in the rush and roar of lower Broadway.

CHAPTER V

THE MESSAGE IN CIPHER

The house to which Chief Flynn had directed the wireless patrol proved to be a private residence on a side street that ran between Central Park and the Hudson River. It was a tall house, standing two stories higher than any other structure in the block. Like most of its neighbors it had evidently seen better days. In places the brownstone front was cracked and great chips had flaked off. The broken stones in the long flight of steps that led up to the first floor were patched with colored cement that had faded so the patches stood out baldly. The brass handrail above the stone balustrade was battered and dirty. Altogether it was not a very attractive looking place.

The old lady who opened the door eyed them sharply.

"A gentleman named Flynn recommended me to your place," said Captain Hardy. "We shall need accommodations for quite a while."

"You must be the gentleman from Washington that he 'phoned me about. You are Captain Hardy?"

"I am."

"Come in," said the landlady cordially. "Any friends of Mr. Flynn's are welcome. Your rooms are ready for you. Mr. Flynn said you wanted to be together, so I have given you the entire top floor."

She led the way up one narrow stairway after another until the party reached the top floor. There she threw open the door to the front room and withdrew.

An exclamation of pleasure burst from the lips of the four boys. The shabby exterior of the house and the dim and dingy hallways through which they had come gave no hint of the cozy comfort that awaited them. The room they now entered was of generous size, with soft gray wallpaper and white woodwork. Along one side ran low, well-filled bookshelves. In the middle of the opposite wall, with fire-making materials already piled in it, was a small open grate, surmounted by an attractive mantel of white woodwork. There were a writing-table, a comfortable couch, and easy chairs. And what was most unusual for a city house, the room possessed windows on three sides—two overlooking the street and one giving a view over the housetops on either side. A door at the rear opened into a second room that was equipped as a writing room, with a broad table and several straight-backed chairs. Here, too, was an open grate set in a white mantel. In the room behind this were a number of cots. Back of all was the bath room. A snugger and more comfortable place it would have been hard to find. But nowhere was there anything that suggested a wireless outfit.

The boys looked at one another questioningly. "He said there was an outfit here," said Lew, "so there must be. But I don't see where it can be."

"It would be somewhere by itself," said Roy, "so that the operator wouldn't be disturbed. It must be on another floor."

"But if we are to keep a twenty-four-hour watch," argued Henry, "it ought to be right in our apartment."

"Let's look at the aerial, anyway," suggested Lew.

A door at the end of the hallway quite evidently led to the roof. They had noticed it as they followed their landlady up the stairs. Willie led the way through it and the boys found themselves on the roof, which, like the roofs of most city houses, was flat. Like its neighbors, also, this roof was encumbered with a number of long, wire clothes-lines, but the boys found nothing that suggested an aerial to them. Puzzled, they returned to their apartment.

Presently there was a rap at the door. Captain Hardy opened it and a man dressed as a waiter, whom they had seen in the hallway as they entered, stepped into the room.

"I came to show you your outfit," he said.

Stepping into the writing room, he grasped the corners of the mantel and gave a sharp pull. The entire upper half of the mantel swung outward and came to rest on the writing-table, revealing a compact but wonderfully well-equipped wireless outfit, including even a wireless detector for telling the direction a wireless message came from. The boys stared in astonishment while the waiter grinned.

"What kind of a boarding-house is this, anyway?" asked Lew.

"This ain't no boardin'-house," replied the man. "This is a sort of headquarters for secret service men from out of town."

"Where's your aerial?" demanded Willie.

Lewis E. Theiss

"If you go on the roof you'll see it—that is you will if your eyes are sharp enough."

"I'll bet it's those wire clothes-lines," said Willie.

"Nothin' wrong with your eyes," said the waiter with a smile. "But I guess there wouldn't be, if the Chief sent you here."

Naturally each of the boys was eager to test the outfit before them. They crowded round it, sliding the coil, shifting the condenser, examining this and that, and voicing their approval and pleasure in the different instruments.

"We may as well begin our watch at once," said Captain Hardy. "Each of you will have to listen in six hours a day. If we divide the watches into two tricks of three hours each, it will be easier for you."

The matter was arranged accordingly, and the first trick given to the most experienced operator, Henry. After the others had seen him take his seat and adjust his receivers to his head, they withdrew from the wireless room.

But Henry was far from being in solitude. Sitting apparently alone, he was listening to a multitude of voices; for before beginning his vigil he wanted to test out his instruments and see how well they worked and how sharply they would register sounds. So he sat at his table, tuning now to this wave length and now to that, now catching a land message and now one from the sea. Distinctly he caught the signal NAA from the great navy wireless plant at Arlington. He recognized it before the operator had finished sending his call signal. Night after night with his home-made outfit at Central City, Henry had heard this station send forth the time signals at ten o'clock; and during his brief period as radio man for Uncle Sam he had often talked with Arlington, both sending and receiving messages from the great station. But though he recognized the voice, he did not know the language he heard; for Arlington was flinging abroad a message in the secret code of the navy. Press messages and commercial communications were buzzing through the air like swarms of bees. Orders to departing steamships came surging over his line. Suddenly a strong whining note filled the air, drowning out all other notes, and Henry knew the Brooklyn Navy Yard was talking. He caught messages from the Waldorf, from the Wanamaker station, from the police wireless. Never had he heard so many messages or imagined that the air could be so filled with talk. And had he not been a very able operator, he would have been so confused by the babel that he would have understood none of it clearly. But he tuned sharply, shutting out interfering vibrations, and caught clearly message after message. But every message that he intercepted was sent by a regularly licensed station.

After he had sufficiently tested his instruments, and assured himself of their ability to register even the faintest sounds sharply and distinctly, Henry shifted his coils and condensers again and began to listen in for messages of less than three hundred meters' wave length. Instantly the room that had hummed with voices grew silent as a cave. No message, no vibrations, no whisper of sound came to his waiting ears. For three hours he sat, continually shifting his coils, but he heard nothing. As well might he have sat three hours by a rock, waiting for it to speak. And well he knew that this was only the first of many long weary watches that would be kept ere the voice they looked for would come out of the air.

Vividly Henry recalled the long vigils at Camp Brady, when he sat for many hours at a time listening for the call of the dynamiters. He remembered how irksome that had been. He remembered the chill of the night and the silence of the great forest. Here the watchers would be more comfortable, but the vigil was likely to be as tedious and trying as their watch in the Pennsylvania mountains had proved. But that watch had been rewarded. The dynamiters had been located and captured. And Henry never doubted that this vigil, too, would meet with success. So he schooled himself to patience and keyed his ear and his instrument to the keenest pitch.

Meantime his companions had lost not a moment in beginning their study of the city. When Captain Hardy emerged from the wireless room, he ran his eye over the contents of the bookshelves; and one section he discovered was filled with maps and guide-books and local histories, not only of New York but also of other American cities. He found a large-scale map of the metropolis and spread it out on the table, true to the indicated compass points. Clustered about this outspread map, the other members of the patrol followed with eager eyes and retentive minds their instructor's every word.

Dr. Hardy called their attention to the contour of Manhattan Island, long and tongue-shaped, and running almost north and south. He showed them the main thoroughfares, the great arteries of north and south traffic. He traced for them the routes of subway, surface, and elevated car lines. Together they located the tunnels and the ferries. They studied the harbor and the different shipping districts, coming quickly to know where the transatlantic liners docked, where the coastwise steamers were berthed, and where tramp steamers could find safe anchorages. They examined the harbor and adjacent waterways. They studied the locations of police stations and hospitals, of passenger stations and freight depots. They noted the location of the forts. They identified the sites of the largest buildings.

When they had finished with Manhattan, they studied one by one the other boroughs—the Bronx, the boroughs east of

Manhattan, Staten Island, and finally the Jersey shore, searching always for what would lend itself to spying or the use of a secret wireless. Especially they studied all that related to ships that cross the Atlantic.

Not in one evening or in one day was this accomplished, but through the long hours of many days, as one boy after another took his turn at the wireless. And between tricks at listening in or studying maps and guide-books, they roamed the streets, traveled on subway and surface and elevated trains, crossed the ferries, rode in the sightseeing motors, visited the bridges, the museums, the public buildings, and within a short time knew more about the topography and geography of the city than nine-tenths of the people who lived in it. As they became accustomed to the noise and the confusion and were able to find their way about with ease, they scraped acquaintances on every side, and soon knew a multitude of newsies, porters, policemen, truck drivers, car-conductors, and others.

Hour after hour, day after day, night after night, they listened in. A week passed. Then another went by. But excepting for one or two snatches of talk, seemingly innocent, the watchers at the wireless caught nothing.

Then, as Roy was listening in one noon while his comrades were down-stairs at luncheon, there was a sudden buzzing in his ear. Rapidly he shifted coil and condenser until the vibrations came sharp and clear. A call was sounding. 2XB was calling 5ZM. Roy seized his pencil and copied the signals, at the same time trying hard to locate the direction from which the signals came. It was well that Roy was a fast operator, for the message that followed came with such rapidity that it taxed Roy's ability to catch it. But he managed to get every letter. When the message was ended, Roy reached for his list of stations and rapidly ran through it. The

Lewis E. Theiss

stations he had overheard were not listed. There could be no doubt about it. He had caught a message from a secret wireless. He turned to the paper with the message. Here is what he had written down: SRPSTSNIAOLTMIXNREHONTSTFIRG. But he could make no sense of it. The letters would not form themselves into words, combine them as he would. He rose and ran to the dining-room with the paper.

Captain Hardy studied it for an instant. "Take this at once to Chief Flynn," he said. "He may want to ask some questions about it. Willie will relieve you at the wireless."

Several hours passed before Roy returned, and Captain Hardy began to fear lest, despite the training in the geography of the city, Roy had become confused and gotten lost. Then suddenly the door of the wireless apartment burst open and Roy flew in.

"Chief Flynn told me he thought his men could unravel that message and that I should wait a while," panted Roy, breathless from running up the stairs. "And they did get it. It's what they call a transposition cipher. Here is what it says."

He held out a sheet of paper. On it the letters Roy had picked out of the air were arranged in four lines, as follows:

S R P S T S N
I A O L T M I
X N R E H O N
T S T F I R G

"Read down instead of across," explained Roy.

Captain Hardy studied the cipher a moment more, then read aloud: "Six transports left this morning."

CHAPTER VI

A NEW DANGER POINT

For a moment there was dead silence. Then Captain Hardy spoke. "You have done excellent work, Roy," he said. "Beyond doubt this is a message from a German spy. It is fortunate you caught this particular message, for it proves that, whether there is a leak in the navy department or not, the Germans are watching our ships here in New York. Did you catch the direction this came from, Roy?"

"Yes, sir. I marked the direction on the blotter beneath the detector."

"We'll take a look at it," said the leader, and the little band entered the wireless room, where Lew was now on duty.

On the white blotter they found a long black line, tipped with an angle mark like an arrow-head. Captain Hardy got a map of the city, and spreading it on the table true to the compass points, stretched a yardstick across it in the direction indicated by the arrow.

"Hoboken," he muttered. "The arrow points to Hoboken." For a moment he studied the map before him. "You will remember," he said, looking up, "that Hoboken is the point on the Jersey side of the Hudson where there are such great railroad freight yards and such huge piers. Many Atlantic liners sail from Hoboken. Evidently the Germans are watching there. Of course they would be. Their spies are informing other German agents every time a troop ship sails. And somehow they get that news to Germany. It's a terrible menace to our army, boys. We must put an end to it."

"We will," came the reply from four sober-faced boys.

"It's going to be a long task, boys," said Captain Hardy. "Get your hats and we'll take a look at Hoboken."

Leaving Lew at the wireless, the four others set out. They rode for a distance on a Ninth Avenue elevated train, then walked to the ferry, and in less than an hour of the time they left their headquarters found themselves in the great Jersey shipping point.

Never had the boys from Central City seen anything quite like the water-front at Hoboken. The level ground was one great maze of railroad tracks, freight depots, warehouses, and pier sheds. The wide thoroughfare running along the waterfront presented a scene of bewildering confusion. Trolley-cars, steam trains, motor trucks, horse-drawn vehicles, and other conveyances were moving this way and that. Whistles were tooting, motors honking, bells ringing, drivers swearing, policemen shouting orders. Pedestrians were dodging in and out, messenger boys were darting here and there. Porters were carrying bundles on their shoulders, laborers were wheeling materials in steel wheelbarrows, lines of heavily laden trucks were passing into steamship piers, and guards and watchmen at every entrance were closely scrutinizing all who approached.

The four observers walked slowly along, studying every foot

of the way. High fences had been built here and there to hide what was going on behind them. Covered ways led from railway terminals to pier sheds so that none could see what had come by train. Even the gangways to the ships were screened. Every precaution had been taken to baffle curious eyes.

"They've done their best," commented Captain Hardy, "but they can't screen a ship on the river, and the Germans know when our transports sail, even if they don't know what's in them. Any one with a good glass can look out from any house along the river front and see clearly every move made by a steamer. Let's take a stroll among these houses."

They left the bustling water-front and passed to the higher ground where stood the city proper. It was like most other American municipalities—dirty, dingy, and unattractive, a hotchpotch of buildings with no architectural unity. But it had one feature possessed by few cities—an outlook on a great and busy harbor.

As the boys stood looking at the rolling Hudson below them, watching the ferry-boats come and go, like huge shuttles in a giant loom, following the movements of steamers, and tugs and tow-boats, and tracing the circling flight of the gulls, they forgot entirely the errand that had brought them. Presently their leader broke the silence.

"We shall have to get to work," he said.

Starting at one end of the street, they walked slowly along its entire length, studying every house that fronted on the river. They saw at once that their task was hopeless. Square after square the houses stretched in unbroken blocks. A hundred spies might be living in those houses and no one be the wiser. A hundred wireless outfits might be flashing messages among the clothes-lines on the roofs and only a roof to roof survey would reveal the fact. But it was not necessary to run even so slender a risk of discovery. As the wireless patrol knew only too well, an aerial would work with great efficiency even though it were strung in a chimney or erected entirely within doors. Yet the little party continued its investigation until dusk, scanning every window whence a glass might be directed toward the river, and threading alleys and scrutinizing the wires of roofs and yards. But nowhere did they see anything to arouse their suspicion.

"We may as well go back, boys," their leader said at last. "We shall have to depend upon our ears rather than our eyes if we are to catch these villains. But we have made progress. We know where they are. We have limited our field of observation to one place. Now we shall have to do as we did at Elk City. We shall have to get two portable sets with compact detectors and begin a watch in Hoboken. We'll have to find this hidden wireless by triangulation, just as we caught the dynamiters. But we haven't enough of a force to maintain two watches. We shall likely have to send for more of the boys to come on."

They recrossed the river and made their way back to their headquarters. Lew had heard nothing. He was relieved by Henry.

The others went down to dinner, and food was sent up to the lone watcher. But when his trick was ended, he made the same report that Lew had rendered. He, too, had heard nothing.

"Doubtless," said Captain Hardy, "they use their wireless seldom for fear of discovery. Probably they send a message only when troop ships have actually sailed. That is likely the reason it was such a long time before we caught the first message. And it may be just as long before we hear another. But when it comes, we must be ready with our two detectors. I'll see Chief Flynn about them in the morning. And I'll tell him what we have learned in addition to what the cipher message told us."

"I wonder," said Roy, "how the secret service men ever unraveled that cipher. I could never have done it. I was looking for something like the code message we caught at Camp Brady."

"It probably was not very difficult, Roy," replied Captain Hardy, "or it could not have been fathomed so soon. I believe that most cipher messages to-day are like the one you caught at Camp Brady. Apparently they are innocent messages but they have a hidden meaning. The most difficult cipher messages, I have heard, are of the substitution kind, where many alphabets are used. It is pretty difficult to decipher such messages unless you have the key word."

"Then why didn't the Germans use a substitution cipher when they sent this message about the transports?" asked Willie. "Then we might never have been able to tell what they said."

"It was hardly worth while, Willie. They know the authorities are listening for their messages. It made no particular difference if the contents of this message were known. But when they send out an order for a spy to do something, I have no doubt they use the most difficult code they can devise, or at least one that they believe only the spy will understand. So we may expect to catch messages in different codes before we are through with our work."

Captain Hardy rose and began to look along the shelves of books. "Here is a volume," he said presently, "that will tell us a great deal about cipher messages."

He had just laid open the book when Roy rushed in from the wireless room. "I've got another message," he said, holding out a paper on which was a long string of letters.

"I wasn't expecting another message so soon," said Captain Hardy in surprise. Slowly he read the letters on the paper Roy had given him:

"FTSTITEIAFTDLLTNSYWTORPSLHVNRLEEYLIOTEI H UAOSEIEGGEVNCENDRRTERNRADSNLEEITOCGEO SHM."

"It looks like the same cipher used before," he went on. "If it is, we can unravel this message without bothering the secret service. At any rate we'll make a try at it. Where's that other message, Willie?"

The first message was brought. Captain Hardy spread it on the table and the group bent over it.

"The letters divide evenly into four lines, you notice," said the leader. "Let's see if this message will do the same."

He counted the letters with his pencil. "Eighty," he announced. "That would make four lines of twenty letters each. We'll try it."

Rapidly he copied the first twenty letters. Below them he made a second line of the next twenty letters. Then the third set of twenty was written down. As he began the fourth row the three boys at his side held their breath.

"He's got it," Willie Brown cried, as Captain Hardy wrote

down the first letter. "He's got it. It spells four."

Rapidly Captain Hardy finished out his line. The letters he had written down read like this:

FTSTITEIAFTDLLTNSYWT
ORPSLHVNRLEEYLIOTEIH
UAOSEIEGGEVNCENDRRTE
RNRADSNLEEITOCGEOSHM

He picked up the paper and slowly spelled out the following message:

"Four—transports—sailed—this—evening— Large—fleet—evidently—collecting— No—destroyers—with—them."

For a moment there was complete silence. Then Henry spoke. "They can see everything in Hoboken," he said. "It's a wonderful place to spy from."

"That message didn't come from Hoboken," said Roy, who had been listening to their conversation with one ear while he kept his receiver at the other. "It was for 5ZM all right, but it was signed 2XC instead of 2XB and the detector doesn't point toward Hoboken."

There was a rush for the wireless room. Captain Hardy seized a map, spread it on the table, and again applied the yardstick, extending it in the direction indicated by the detector. The stick pointed straight toward the Narrows, at the entrance to the harbor.

"That message came from Staten Island," said Captain Hardy with conviction. "They have got two secret stations."

CHAPTER VII

CONFUSION WORSE CONFOUNDED

As the possibility of this new difficulty rose before them, the members of the wireless patrol were almost staggered. They knew how difficult it had been to locate the hidden wireless in the mountains at the Elk City storage reservoir, where there were no other wireless plants to distract them and no houses to conceal the apparatus. The obstacles now before them appeared almost insuperable.

The silence was broken by their leader. "I suppose we shall not learn anything, but at least it will be better to look the ground over. So in the morning we'll run over to Staten Island."

Morning found Henry on the wireless watch. Lew's trick was to follow. The two others and Captain Hardy left the house immediately after their breakfast and set off for Staten Island. In order to see something of the city as they journeyed, they went on the Ninth Avenue elevated road, and in half an hour found themselves at South Ferry, whence the city-owned ferry-boats leave for Staten Island. It was their first visit to this ferry and they were impressed by the fine waiting-rooms and the magnificent ferry-boats.

The trip down the harbor thrilled them with pleasure. The narrow channel between Manhattan Island and Governor's Island seemed to be filled with snorting tugboats, strings of barges, great floats carrying many loaded freight-cars, puffing steamships, and even sailing vessels. Whistles were tooting on every side as pilots signaled to one another.

"I don't see how they ever manage to keep from smashing into one another," said Willie as he stood with wide eyes, watching the rapidly moving craft about him.

"They don't always," said Captain Hardy. "But accidents are surprisingly few."

Hardly had they gotten up speed before they passed close to Governor's Island, the military reservation which was the army headquarters for the Department of the East. With great interest they looked at Castle William, the great circular stone fort, now useless for protection, but venerable with age and tradition, that stood at the western edge of the island.

Soon they were past the island and out in the open bay. Far to the left were the Brooklyn shores, with their great shipping terminals and stores and clustered steamers. On the right, and still more distant, ran the low Jersey coast, almost hidden in fog and smoke. Against this dull background towered the Statue of Liberty. Reverently the boys stood looking at this great image, known the world over as no other statue is known, and symbolic of all a free earth holds dear—symbolic of that liberty, fraternity, equality that the free men of the world are giving their lives to preserve. A mist rose in their eyes as they looked at this symbol of that which they, too, were giving their devoted efforts to preserve—their homes, their families, their freedom. And on every face came a set expression of determination that, even though the countenances wearing it were youthful, boded no good to the treacherous enemies of freedom whose trail they were that very moment following. Then they flashed past Robbin's Reef light and snuggled into their slip at Staten Island.

Before them towered the community of St. George, straggling, like some old world village, up the sloping streets to the heights. Quickly they climbed a winding road that led to the top of the hill. Like Jerusalem the golden, the village about them was beautiful for situation. For miles it commanded an unobstructed view in almost every direction. To the north were the rolling reaches of the Upper Bay across which they had come, with the tall sky-scrapers of Manhattan towering heavenward in the background and looking so near at hand that it was hard to believe that they were six miles distant. Shaped not unlike a pear, the great Bay tapered to stem-like dimensions as it flowed to the east of Staten Island and found its way to that greater sheet of water, the Lower Bay. On the opposite side of this passage rose the bluff shores of Brooklyn. But the Staten Island shore towered high above everything else. On opposite sides of the narrowest parts of the channel to the sea were forts. And it was to this very Narrows that the wireless detector had pointed when Roy caught the message on the previous night.

"From somewhere in this neighborhood that message came," said Captain Hardy. "And beyond a doubt it came from some house on the slope before us. From this view-point an observer can see everything that takes place in both Upper and Lower Bay and spy on every vessel passing through the Narrows. With a powerful glass an observer on these slopes could almost distinguish the buttons on the sailors' clothes or read the compass on the bridge of a ship. Let us see what we can find."

For a mile or two they walked leisurely along the brow of the hill, carefully examining every house that possessed a good outlook over the Narrows. They found many such, but as was the case in Hoboken, the houses were as like as so many peas. In location or construction there was nothing that would direct the finger of suspicion to one house rather than another. Any house with an unobstructed outlook might harbor a spy.

When they had gone far enough along the brow of the hill Captain Hardy said, "Let us go back along the slope. I suspect any observer would get as near to the water as he could and yet have sufficient elevation for a wide view. I believe the place we are looking for is somewhere below us."

They climbed down to a lower level and began their return walk. On the slope the buildings were not so close together. There were more open spaces, more undeveloped stretches where trees yet remained and thickets of underbrush still stood undisturbed.

"These houses would make better radio stations than those so closely crowded together, I should think," commented Captain Hardy.

Slowly they sauntered along, stopping near every suspicious house, ostensibly to view the landscape, and giving it a searching examination as they took in the view. And so artfully was their work done that no one watching the eager group, looking now here, now there, would have dreamed that ships and shipping were the last things they were interested in.

Slowly they worked their way along the slope, now climbing to higher levels, now descending to lower, as it became necessary to view a habitation from one side or the other. But search as they might, nothing stood out in any place that was of a suspicious nature. There were no questionable wire clothes-lines, for here every one seemed to use cotton lines. No flagpoles rose aloft, up which antennas wires could be hoisted in the guise of halyards. No kites flew from back yards. No lightning-rods rose suspiciously above the housetops. There were no tall chimneys inside which hidden wires might be stretched. Nowhere was there anything at which they could definitely point the finger of suspicion.

Almost had they given up hope of finding anything that would help them, when they came to a place where the slope jutted out sharply for a little space, like the nose on a human face. The ground sloped outward for a distance at a gentle angle, then dropped precipitously many feet. But on either side of the nose of land the even slope of the hill was unbroken, just as human cheeks continue their uninterrupted slope from the forehead. Perched on this nose of land was an inconspicuous little house. As the surrounding land was too steep for habitation, this house stood by itself, the slope for many yards on either side being overgrown with bushes and undergrowths, while a considerable stand of pines grew at one side. The fenced-in yard of this house was large, and by an ingenious system of curves a roadway had been built from the public thoroughfare up to the little house. Evidently the owner possessed a motor-car, for a tiny garage was snuggled into the hill beside the dwelling.

But the thing that at once attracted the little patrol was the view afforded by the location. Indeed it was *the* view-point strategically; for the jutting nose of land gave an unobstructed outlook toward both Bays which could be had from no other location on the same level, while the Narrows lay immediately below the house and so close that it seemed as though one could throw a stone from the little house into the water.

For several minutes the three searchers stared at the structure before them. "I believe," said Willie, in the language of blind man's buff, "that we are getting hot."

"Let's look at the place from the other side," suggested Roy.

Slowly they sauntered along the highway, now examining the Narrows, now watching some ship in the offing, but gradually working their way to the other side of the little house. Everywhere except at the rear of the building, where the hill rose steeply, ornamental rows of windows had been built into the structure, giving an uninterrupted view, north, east, and south.

"I'll bet there are no partition walls in that floor," said Roy, "and if there aren't, anybody could sit in the front of the house and look in three directions by merely turning his head. Why that place is just made for spying on shipping."

"And it's exactly where our wireless pointed," said Willie.

"I wonder how we could get into the place and examine it."

"You mustn't think of such a thing," said Captain Hardy. "If there is a wireless outfit there, you may be sure that it will be as effectually secreted as the one in our rooms is, and you would never find it. But you would certainly alarm the people in the house, and the Chief warned me that under no circumstances should we alarm the people we are watching. We must get a complete case against them before any move is made."

"But if this is a wireless station, how are we going to know it unless we search the house?" demanded Roy.

"We shall have to keep a watch on the house itself and try to

Lewis E. Theiss

trail everybody who goes in or out. And we shall keep up our wireless watch. If messages are coming from here we shall run them down just as we intended to run down the Hoboken messages. This place is so much better for spy work, being near the forts as well as the waterways, that we'll drop Hoboken and centre our efforts here. But I don't know just how we'll do it. I'll have to let the Chief outline the plan. We may have to move down here. But in the meantime you boys can keep the place under observation very easily from some of these thickets."

The three went on down the road and passed out of sight of the house, laying their plans as they went. Arrived at the road to the ferry, they separated, Captain Hardy continuing on down to the wharf, while Willie and Roy turned about and retraced their steps. While Captain Hardy was speeding back to Manhattan to consult the secret service men, the two young scouts made their way to a turn of the road whence they could barely see a gable of the house on the cliff. They had not met a soul. They left the highway and scrambled up the slope to a dense thicket of underbrush. Screened by this, they cautiously approached the house and made their way unseen into the little stand of pines they had previously noted.

The cover was good. The pines on the outer edges of the stand, where the light was ample, branched close to the ground, making a dense hedge. Behind these protecting branches the two boys could move freely without fear of discovery. By mounting upward a little distance, they had a perfect view of the house they were watching, and could see all who entered or left it. They found some limbs where they could sit comfortably and took up their vigil.

"Captain Hardy said we must trail anybody who came out of the house," said Willie. "If we follow them on the road we could be seen and we might be suspected. How can we trail them without being seen?"

They looked around. Higher up the slope ran another road, so hidden by shrubbery and bushy growths as to be almost invisible from below. A person walking along this road could easily follow one on the highway below without being seen. A brief study of the slope also showed them a bushy way by which they could scramble unseen up to this road.

Now they gave their undivided attention to the house before them, studying every feature of house and grounds that they might be able, if it became necessary, to make their way safely about the premises. But no one came to the house, no one left it, no one appeared at a window, and there was no sign whatever that a living being was in the house.

The minutes began to drag. It was uninteresting to sit and scrutinize a house when there was so much of real interest to see. So between glances at the home on the cliff, the scouts began to study anew the wonderful harbor that so fascinated them.

Again they studied those distant sky-scrapers, which looked, at the distance, like dream buildings, deceptive structures of the clouds. The waters intervening were palpitant with life. As an hour passed, and then another, the young watchers gave more and more attention to the landscape and less to the house near by. The air was vibrant with the tooting of whistles. The wind was sweeping the water before it in graceful waves. The passing steamers churned it into yeasty foam. Great sailing ships came surging in from the deeps, deck-laden with heavy cargoes, parting the water with their high bows, their sails bellying in the breeze and shining white in the sun. Tugs passed restlessly to and fro, dragging behind them long strings of coal barges. And once a great ocean liner came in through the Narrows, making the very hills vibrate with the thunder of her whistle. Intently the boys watched her as she slowed at quarantine and the port physicians boarded her. By mere chance Willie turned his glance toward the house on the cliff, and there, close to the front windows, stood a man with field-glasses to his eyes, studying the liner in the Narrows below.

"Look!" gasped Willie. "There's a man in the window!"

But before Roy could turn his head the figure had disappeared.

"We almost missed him," said Willie. "We're poor scouts to forget what we are about."

They centred their gaze on the near-by house. Forgotten was the glorious picture spread before them, forgotten everything but the glass-fronted dwelling and the invisible man with the field-glasses. But look as they would, they could see nothing further of a suspicious nature. Another hour passed. Dinner time had long gone by. The one o'clock whistle had blown. And their own stomachs told them accurately what time it was; but they would not leave their post. Now that they had once scented their quarry, as it were, or believed that they had, they were like hounds on the trail. Their training at Camp Brady now showed its effect.

But the hours passed, the afternoon waned, and nothing further occurred to draw their attention to the little house. Gradually their vigilance relaxed. Their eyes wandered again to that fascinating harbor scene, to the never-ending moving picture spread before them. Again they saw tugs and ferry-boats plying busily back and forth, and the flashing sails of great schooners. But presently they saw something like nothing they had ever beheld. Far in the distance was a line of moving objects, gliding through the waves in stately fashion, approaching one behind the other at equal distances. Just what was approaching the two scouts could not at first determine, so indistinct in outline were the moving bulks. But presently, as the oncoming objects drew nearer, the watchers saw that they were great ships. But they looked unlike any ships they had ever seen or heard of. They seemed to be of no color and of every color. They were streaked and splotched in the most curious way. They looked as though some giant hand had flung eggs of different colors against their sides.

The boys looked at one another in astonishment. "Well, what in the mischief ails those boats?" demanded Roy.

They were silent a moment, becoming more amazed than ever.

"I know," cried Willie suddenly. "They're camouflaged. They must be transports." He turned his head for a glance at the house. "Quick!" he said. "There's the man at the window again."

For some minutes the figure before them stood motionless except for the movement of his field-glasses, with which he swept the oncoming fleet of transports. Then he drew back from the window again. The boys kept their eyes fastened on the little house. For a long time nothing occurred. Then a grocer's boy came in sight, struggling up the highway with a basket of supplies on his arm. The watchers paid small attention to him until he turned suddenly into the driveway leading up to the house. A moment later he had disappeared within the building.

"He's only a grocery boy," said Roy.

"We'll have to watch him, anyway," said Willie. "I'll follow him when he comes out and you watch the house."

They had not long to wait. In a few minutes the boy came out, his basket empty, and went skipping down the hill. Quick as a flash Willie scrambled to the roadway above, and, screened by the shrubbery, followed on the higher level. A quarter mile toward the ferry the two highways came together. Willie reached the intersection at almost the same time as the grocer's boy. Each took a glance at the other and kept on his way, Willie dropping a few yards behind the other lad.

A quarter of a mile further on the slope changed and the district was thickly built up. The errand boy soon entered a store. Willie had just time for a quick glance at the sign on the window. It read, "Fritz Berger, Fancy Groceries." Then Willie opened the door and followed the errand boy into the place.

A florid, burly man with upturned mustaches stood behind the counter. The errand boy was talking to him. In his hand he held a silver dollar.

"Here is the money for Mr. Baum's sugar," he was saying.

"Good!" said the grocer, seizing the coin, which he dropped in his pocket. Then he turned to Willie. "Well?" he said inquiringly.

"Sugar," said Willie. "I want five pounds of sugar."

"I have no more," said the grocer. "It is all sold."

"Pshaw!" said Willie. "Where can I get some?"

"I don't know," said the grocer.

"Got any candy?" asked Willie.

"Sure. In that case."

Willie walked to the show-case and slowly examined the stock. "Give me ten cents' worth of those chocolates," he finally ordered.

The storekeeper weighed out the candy and dumped it in a bag. He took the proffered dime, dropped it in his till, and turned away.

Willie left the store and stood for a moment undecided as to which way to go. "Nothing doing there," he said to himself. Then he turned a corner and started down the hill. The supper hour was approaching. People were coming up the street from the ferry, homeward bound from Manhattan. A motor-car came chugging up the road and drew close to the curb. The driver turned his car about, clamped on the brake, and stepped out, leaving his engine running. Willie went on down the street and was soon in the midst of a throng coming up from the ferry. He stopped to look at a jeweler's clock, turned about, and started on his way to rejoin Roy. Suddenly he heard the softly whistled signal of the wireless patrol. He turned sharply about and saw Captain Hardy across the street. He dodged a motor-car that was rooming down the hill and crossed to his captain. There had been no sign of life about the little house since the grocer's boy came out.

"Come," said the leader. "I have seen the Chief and he is going to arrange it so that we can watch this place in comfort. We will go back home now."

They climbed cautiously to the road above. "By George!" exclaimed Captain Hardy suddenly. "You boys haven't had a bite to eat since breakfast. I forgot all about that."

"How about yourself?" asked Roy.

"Well, I haven't either, but that's different. I've had a chance to get something if I had thought of it. We won't wait until we get home to eat. There's a restaurant at the ferry-house. We'll have a good dinner there."

More than an hour passed before the three rose from their table. Another hour had gone by before they reached their headquarters. They were tired and sleepy. But their drowsiness vanished when Henry rushed into the living-room of their apartment and thrust a sheet of paper into Captain Hardy's hands.

"It's another message," he said, "and we deciphered it ourselves."

Captain Hardy stepped to the light and read the message aloud. "Five more transports sailed late this afternoon. All camouflaged."

"We know the man who sent that message," cried Willie. "We've been watching him all the afternoon, down on the hillside at Staten Island."

"But this message didn't come from Staten Island," said Henry. "The detector points straight east over Brooklyn, and the message was sent from a long way off. It was very faint."

CHAPTER VIII

WHERE MONEY TALKED

For a full minute the members of the wireless patrol stared at one another in speechless amazement. Then Willie broke the silence.

"I don't care where it came from," he said. "I just know that the man we were watching sent it."

"But how could he have sent it, when the wireless pointed to Brooklyn?" demanded Henry.

"Oh! I don't mean that he actually sent it with his own fingers," said Willie. "But we saw him watching the ships and there isn't any other place in the whole harbor where you can get such a good view of them. I just know he had something to do with that message."

"I'll bet the Germans have got a string of wireless outfits and that what he does is to stay in that house and spy on ships that pass through the Narrows and then telephone to one of these secret wireless stations," said the nimble-witted Roy. "And if that's the case he hasn't any wireless at all himself."

"If Roy is right," said Henry, "it's a pretty clever scheme.

Lewis E. Theiss

The secret service could take his house to pieces and not find a wire in it. Yet he's the man that's sending the messages, or at least starting them."

"Roy is doubtless correct," said their leader. "We know they have at least three stations and they may have many more. The object of that, of course, is to baffle any wireless man who may be on their track. If we hadn't stumbled on this spy post at Staten Island, we should have been completely blocked ourselves. But we've got something definite to work on now. We've got a definite clue. And sooner or later we will uncover some of their hidden stations. From now on we've got to watch this man on Staten Island as well as listen for messages. I don't see how we are to do it unless we send for more of the boys or move to Staten Island."

When the matter was laid before Chief Flynn he said no more boys were needed. Too many boys in one house would attract attention. So he arranged to transfer the wireless patrol to Staten Island. Living on the slope above the suspected house was a well-to-do but childless couple with a rather large house, who were warm friends of the Chief's; and they readily agreed, as a matter of service to their country, to take the wireless patrol into their home. So a wireless outfit was installed, with a concealed aerial, and the boys found themselves situated even more pleasantly than they had been before.

And it was well that they were pleasantly situated, for though their task was not difficult in one sense, in another it was extremely trying. Six hours a day each boy sat at the wireless listening in. Had it been possible to tune to longer wave lengths and pick up the interesting news with which the air was fairly alive, the task would have been anything but irksome. But to sit hour after hour with their instruments tuned to the short wave lengths used by the German agents and hear nothing, was trying enough. The watch on the spy's nest proved hardly less tedious. From a gable-window in the attic a very fair view could be had of the little house below. Here, on rainy days, a watcher sat during all the hours of daylight; and on other days the sheltering pines hid an observer. But day followed day, night succeeded night, and no message was registered on the wireless instrument nor did anything suspicious occur in the house under surveillance.

Indeed the fact that nothing did occur was in itself suspicious. For there was hardly a sign of life about the house. No man left it in the morning bound for business. No woman emerged from its door to go shopping of an afternoon. For days at a time nobody entered or left the place, excepting the grocer's boy who came with food.

Then one day a motor-car, with its top raised, chugged up the highway and climbed the steep driveway to the house on the cliff. Henry was in the attic gable on watch and he promptly notified his comrades. There was a rush for the third story, and four heads crowded close together as four pairs of eyes sought to identify the make and number of the car. But the name-plate was missing, and the license tag was so dusty that the number could not be read.

"Run down to the pines with this, quick," said Captain Hardy, thrusting his field-glasses into Willie's hand, "and get the number of that car. See if you can tell what make it is and look for distinguishing marks."

Willie scrambled down the slope through the concealing shrubbery and approached the house as near as he dared. But he had hardly reached his station when the driver ran down the steps of the house, sprang to the wheel, and was off at a fast pace. Willie climbed cautiously back to headquarters.

"Did you get its number?" asked his chief.

"No," replied Willie. "It was covered with dust. And I couldn't tell what make of car it was. But I saw the driver and I am sure I have seen him before and the car, too."

"That's not unlikely," said Captain Hardy, "if he lives anywhere near here. We've been here several days now."

"I'm sure I've seen that man somewhere," said Willie. "I wish I could remember where it was."

Another day passed and another, and still the little house on the cliff showed no signs of life. But one afternoon the monotonous watch came to a sudden end. Lew, in the attic gable, espied a fleet of transports coming down the bay. Instantly he spread the alarm.

"You boys slip down to the pines," said Captain Hardy to Willie and Roy. "If any one comes out of the house trail him. Now we'll find out whether this spy—if he be a spy— telephones his news or sends it out by messenger. The Chief has had the telephone wires tapped and is receiving a record of all conversations."

Lew continued his watch aloft. Henry sat tense at the wireless, waiting to catch any possible message, and Roy and Willie scrambled cautiously down to their favorite observation post in the pines. On came the transports, riding the waves in a stately column; yet the little house seemed as lifeless as ever.

"Watch close," whispered Willie. "Don't let anything escape us."

On came the ships, nearer and nearer, throwing the white

spray away from their bows. They passed Robbin's Reef light. They drew close to the entrance to the Narrows. Breathlessly the boys awaited their nearer approach. The transports reached the narrowest part of the passage and still there was no sign of life in the little house. Willie gave a sigh of disappointment and started to speak; but before he could utter a word there was a movement in the window before them and the man they had previously seen appeared for a moment sweeping the Narrows with his glasses. Then he disappeared from sight.

"It's him!" exclaimed Willie, forgetting his grammar in his excitement. "Now he's either telephoning his message or getting it ready for a messenger. We'll soon know."

They had not long to wait. A figure was seen coming up the highway.

"It's only the grocer's boy," said Willie in disappointment. "This is the time he usually comes."

"I wonder if we aren't on a wild-goose chase," said Roy. "Maybe the man in that house isn't any spy at all. I begin to think so."

"I don't," maintained Willie. "I just know he's a spy, but how he sends his messages I can't figure out."

Just then the grocer's boy came out of the house. "There's no use trailing him," said Roy. "We already know who he is. While we're following him the messenger might come—if there is one."

"Captain Hardy said we should follow any one who left the house," said Willie, "so I suppose we'll have to watch this errand boy. You go this time, Roy."

Lewis E. Theiss

In a minute Roy had reached the higher thoroughfare. He ran down the road at top speed and got to the grocery store before the loitering errand boy even came up into this higher road from the lower thoroughfare. But instead of entering the store, Roy turned the corner, retracing his steps in time to enter the store half a minute before the errand boy got there.

The grocer was behind the counter. "Have you any crackers?" asked Roy.

The grocer took down a package of Uneeda biscuits.

"You don't have any loose ones?" asked Roy.

"No, these are all we keep."

"Guess I'll have to take 'em," said Roy. "Got any candy?"

"In the case there," was the answer.

Roy walked over to the show-case and began to examine the stock. Just then the errand boy came in.

"Here's the money for the sugar," he said, handing the grocer a silver dollar.

The grocer took the coin and carelessly dropped it into his pocket.

Roy continued his inspection of the stock of sweetmeats. "Give me five cents' worth of gum-drops," he said.

The grocer began to weigh them out. A tall man with gauntlets and with motor goggles on his forehead came in.

"Hello, Fritz," he said jovially. "Got that sugar for me yet?"

"Just sold my last ounce," said the grocer. "I haven't been able to get a bit for three days."

"Himmel!" said the customer. "How much longer have I got to go without sugar in my coffee?"

He turned to go.

"Hello!" called the grocer. "Here's that dollar I owe you."

The man turned back, and the grocer pulled the coin from his pocket and dropped it into the man's gloved hand.

"Good luck to you," he said, then finished weighing out the gum-drops for Roy, and dropped the nickel in his cash drawer.

Slowly Roy retraced his steps. "Well, what happened?" asked Willie, as Roy rejoined him.

"Nothing," said Roy in disgust. "The errand boy came in and handed the grocer a dollar that he had collected for sugar. Pretty soon an automobile driver came in to get some sugar and the grocer said he hadn't any more, but he paid him a dollar he owed him."

Willie was silent, turning the matter over in his mind. "Then what?" he asked after a time.

"Nothing, except that I bought some candy and the grocer put the money in his cash drawer. Then I left."

"Where else would he put it?" asked Willie, abstractedly, as he tried to read some meaning into the grocer's apparently meaningless acts.

Lewis E. Theiss

"Well," said Roy, "he didn't put the dollar the errand boy gave him into the drawer. He dropped that into his pocket."

"Why, that's exactly what happened when I was in there the other day," said Willie in surprise.

The daylight waned. Dusk came on. It grew too dark to see the spy's house from the pines. It was past time to relieve Henry at the wireless. The two scouts climbed to their own house for orders. As they came up the stairs they heard the voice of Henry.

"Come quick," he called. "I've got another message."

Everybody rushed to Henry's side. Captain Hardy seized the sheet of paper from Henry's hand, and counted the long string of letters written on it. Quickly he rearranged them in four equal lines. Then slowly he read the cipher. "Another transport fleet assembling. First five boats went to sea this afternoon."

"Where did this message come from?" he demanded, as he laid down the paper.

"From some point down the Jersey coast," said Henry, "and probably not more than twenty miles away."

A long silence followed. "We're simply up against it," said Lew dejectedly. "We don't get anywhere."

Suddenly Willie jumped to his feet with a cry. "I've got it! I've got it!" he almost shouted. "Why didn't I see it before?"

"Got what?" asked Roy, astonished.

Willie paid no attention to his question. "What sort of a

looking man was that motorist?" he cried.

"A tall fellow, with black hair and with a big scar on his cheek," said the astonished Roy.

"I knew it," cried Willie. "I knew it! Now I know how the messages are carried. It's as plain as can be."

His fellows clustered about him. "What do you mean?" said Captain Hardy eagerly. "Explain."

"Well," said Willie, "when I followed that grocer's boy the other day, I saw him give the grocer a dollar which he said he had collected for sugar. The grocer put it in his pocket. But when I gave him money for candy he dropped it in his till. Just after I left the store and turned the corner a man drove up in a motor. I noticed him because he turned his car completely around and stopped at the curb. He got out and left his engine running. When I crossed the street to meet you, after you whistled, I dodged a motor-car. It was the same car, but I thought nothing of it." He paused, as though collecting his thoughts.

"Go on," said their leader eagerly.

"To-day," resumed Willie, "Roy followed that same grocer's boy from the house on the cliff to the grocery store and saw him give the grocer a dollar, which he said he had collected for sugar. The grocer dropped the coin in his pocket, but he put Roy's nickel in his drawer. A minute later an automobile driver came in. The grocer said he owed him a dollar and gave him the coin from his pocket. That driver was the same one I saw the other day."

"How do you know?" interrupted Captain Hardy. "You didn't see him to-day?"

Lewis E. Theiss

"But Roy saw him. He's a tall man with black hair and with a scar on his left cheek. That's the man I saw, and it's the man who drove up to the house on the cliff the other day. I knew that I had seen him, but I couldn't remember just where." For a moment he stood silent, fairly panting with excitement.

"Well?" said Lew. "What about him? The grocer could owe him a dollar as well as anybody."

"But he didn't owe him a dollar," cried Willie. "Don't you see? The spy in the house below gave that dollar to the errand boy. He gave it to the grocer. He gave it to the motor driver. It's the same dollar. He didn't put it in the till with the other coins. He kept it in his pocket separate. That automobile driver is the man who carried the messages to the wireless. The messages are on the dollars."

CHAPTER IX

A FRESH START

Amazed, the members of the little patrol looked at one another silently.

"How could they send a message on a dollar?" demanded Lew at last. "They'd have to engrave it, and then they'd never dare to use the dollar again. Besides, it would be too dangerous. If the message were on paper, the paper could be burned or chewed up and swallowed, and the evidence of crime destroyed. But they couldn't erase the engraving on a dollar."

"I don't know how they do it," said Willie, "but I'm sure they write their messages on those dollars."

"Willie is doubtless right," said Captain Hardy. "We don't know how they do it, but the evidence leads directly to the conclusion Willie has come to. The spy in the house below us writes his messages on dollars and sends them through this grocer's boy and the motor-car driver to the various secret wireless plants the Germans evidently possess near New York. I think that is plain. And it indicates new lines of action for us. We must not only continue to listen in for messages and watch this spy's nest, but we shall have to follow this motor-car driver and also learn the secret of the dollars."

"Hurrah!" cried Roy, his eyes shining. "Now there'll be something doing." Then he struck a tragic attitude and declaimed, "Little do the treacherous hawks in yonder nest realize that the eagles of the law are about to swoop down on them."

"Some orator, Roy," said Lew. "If we're eagles, we must have wings. Are mine sprouting yet?" And he turned his back to Roy for the latter's examination.

When the laughter ceased, their leader went on, "You boys are to be congratulated for your discovery. You have accomplished a great deal. But what has been done is little compared with what remains to be done. And so far you have worked in safety. The work ahead may be very dangerous. The hidden wireless stations we are after are probably in lonely places. The men operating them are desperate fellows and will not hesitate even to commit murder. If one of you boys should follow this motor driver into a lonesome spot and then be caught, you might never return."

The smiles faded from the faces before him. But the grave looks that succeeded were not expressions of fear. Rather they were looks of determination—the same set marks of grim purpose that Captain Hardy had seen on these same youthful faces when the wireless patrol was stalking the desperate dynamiters at the Elk City reservoir.

Again it was Roy who brought back the smiles. "If we have to follow that automobile driver," he said, "it's a question of 'where do we go from here, boys?'"

"Only the boy who does the following can answer that question," answered Captain Hardy. "But there are several matters that we can decide at once. I think that we've determined pretty definitely that the man in the house below us—"

"In the hawk's nest," interrupted Roy.

"Well, the man in the hawk's nest," continued their leader, smiling, "is a German spy, that he is there to report the movements of our transports, and that he does it by means of messages sent out on silver dollars. Now we've got to get hold of one of those dollars. That might not be a difficult task in itself. We could hold up the grocer's boy and take the dollar away from him, or we might get it away from him by trickery and substitute another dollar for the stolen one. We might even be able to pick the grocer's pocket and give him a substitute coin. But neither plan would help us because the trick would soon be discovered and the spies would know that they are suspected. It wouldn't do us any good to get their code if they knew we had it. They would simply use another. What we must do is to locate their agents, one after another, learn their codes and ciphers, and catch their messages in the air. When we have laid bare the entire scheme and learned who their agents are, then the secret service can grab the entire organization at once and end this treachery for good."

Captain Hardy paused and looked uneasily across the room, as though lost in thought. His companions were quiet as mice, each also busy with his own thoughts.

"It's a long, hard task, boys," said the captain, after a time, and he drew a deep breath, "a long task and, from now on, a dangerous task. Whatever you do, boys, remember the Chief's warning. Above all else, we must be careful not to

Lewis E. Theiss

alarm the men we are watching."

As Captain Hardy rose to get his hat he said, "I don't quite see how we are to follow this motor-car driver without being detected. So I am going over to Manhattan to see the agent the Chief has put in charge of this investigation. Perhaps I'll have some interesting news for you when I return. Meantime, keep your eyes and ears open and be careful."

With renewed interest and determination the members of the wireless patrol returned to their posts. But though they listened faithfully at the wireless and uninterruptedly watched the hawk's nest on the cliff below them, no alarming sound came out of the air and no suggestive movement occurred within their vision.

Their captain came back with a smile of satisfaction on his face. But the members of the wireless patrol were too well disciplined to question their leader. They knew that, as always before, he would give them the proper orders at the proper time; and that if they obeyed those orders faithfully and intelligently, success would follow. But Captain Hardy was different in many respects from other commanders, and his subordinates were not at all like ordinary privates in an army. There was no question as to their loyalty, discretion, or intelligence; and their leader believed he could attain the greatest success by taking them into his confidence. So presently he answered the question that each boy was longing to ask.

From his pocket he produced detailed maps of all the neighboring country, so mounted on cheese-cloth, after being cut into squares, that they could be folded into small size without injuring the maps themselves. Thus the bearer could always follow his route, whether he walked or rode, whether the air was calm or the wind blew fiercely, by carrying in his hand the necessary map folded in small compass.

Now Captain Hardy spread out his maps full length on a table, and for half an hour the little group bent over them, heads close together, examining the topography of the city's environs as once they had studied the city itself. Marked to show altitudes, roads, byways, rivers, streams, marshes, woodlands, and even the buildings themselves, these maps enabled the little group of scouts to see, through their imaginations, every foot of the country about New York.

They visualized the great, flat, low-lying stretches of southern Long Island and New Jersey; the abrupt bluffs of Long Island's northern coast by the shore of the Sound; the various watery arms that encircle the American metropolis, permitting ships to sail in every direction; the majestic Hudson leading straight north through a wonderful country of rocks and hills, the impressive Palisades flanking its western bank with their towering perpendicular walls of stone; and the rocky, rolling country lying west of them, interspersed with streams and swamps and woodlands and open fields and clustered villages. And when they had finished their study of the maps, they knew more about the topography of the country they had studied, its roads and paths and groves and elevations and other physical characteristics, than half the people who lived in the region. So they were prepared, if need be, to find their way about with little difficulty. And it was well they were so prepared. In the dangerous days to come they were to need all this knowledge.

When they had studied the maps to their hearts' content—and each of the four boys again and again examined them— Captain Hardy folded the maps and thrust them into a water-proof cover. They made a neat little packet like a thin book.

"You will be interested to learn what the secret service has found out," said Captain Hardy, as he stowed the maps in his pocket. "When I left here, I reported immediately to the man in charge of this particular investigation. Our discovery seems to me so important that I ventured to ask why the secret service men didn't take the case up themselves, as they would no doubt get along much faster than we possibly can. For it seems to me message sending ought to be stopped at once. The agent said that all this was true, but that the secret service was so crowded with work it had to take up the most important matters first."

"Most important matters!" cried Roy, in indignation. "Doesn't the secret service consider the guarding of our troops important?"

"Yes, Roy. But whether the Germans know exactly when our ships leave or not, their submarines will be waiting for them and our destroyers will always be guarding the transports. But here in New York German spies are trying to create riots, to blow up buildings, to burn factories. They destroyed almost a million bushels of wheat in one fire recently. So you see that the secret service first must watch the enemies that are trying to destroy our greatest city. Our secret service isn't one-quarter as large as it should be. That is the fault of Congress. But meantime it is doing wonderful work, and it is a great privilege to be able to assist in that work."

"But what have they found out about this job?" demanded Roy.

"You're like a hound on a keen scent, Roy," said their leader. "Nothing ever takes you away from your objective. Well, this is what they've found. It seems that they have been keeping a record of the grocer's telephone messages, as well as those from the 'hawk's nest' down below. Every time transports sail, some one in Hoboken calls up this grocer and says, 'I have some sugar on the way. Do you want any?' And the grocer replies, 'Yes. How many barrels can you let me have?' And the man in Hoboken gives the number. That number corresponds with the number of transports about to sail. So you see how the grocer knows when to send his boy for the wireless messages. But before he sends him, he always telephones to the 'hawk's nest' and says, 'I have some sugar coming and can let you have five pounds to-day. Do you want it?' And the number of pounds he offers is the same as the number of ships that are to sail. So the spy below us knows what to look for. And I suppose the man in Hoboken also telephones the automobile driver when to come for the dollars."

"Who is this man in Hoboken that does the telephoning?" demanded Roy, when Captain Hardy had done speaking.

"Ah! That they don't know. He has always called up from a different place and has gotten away before the secret service could spot him. But the agent assures me that they'll have him soon. He always telephones from a station close to the piers where the transports load. The next time he calls for the grocer, the telephone operator is going to delay him while she notifies a secret service agent posted near by with a motor-cycle. So they'll spot him and trail him.

"And that reminds me," continued Captain Hardy, after a pause, "that we're to do a little motor-cycle work ourselves, and that Henry has been selected for the job because he is familiar with motor-cycles."

Henry's eyes lighted with pleasure. Not only was he the oldest boy in the wireless patrol, and Captain Hardy's first lieutenant, but he was one of those natural mechanics who seem to know instinctively how to handle tools and make things. Indeed he had constructed his own wireless outfit and shown his fellows how to make theirs; and he could repair a motor-cycle almost as skilfully as a garage man. So it was natural that he should be selected for this task.

But there was still another reason why his captain had chosen him for the work he had in mind. Though not so quick or clever as Roy, Henry was a keen observer and close reasoner. Moreover, he was entirely dependable, was very discreet, and being the largest boy in the party, was best fitted to take care of himself if he got into trouble.

"We are going to trail this automobile driver with a motor-cycle, as you have probably guessed," explained Captain Hardy to the little group of scouts. "And Henry is to do the trailing. Come, Henry. We'll go take a look at your machine. The secret service people said that it would be here in half an hour."

"Where? In this house?" asked Roy eagerly.

"No, not here, but at a house around the corner from the grocer's. It will always be in readiness for instant use."

As Henry put on his hat and followed his leader, the other scouts looked at him somewhat enviously. "Remember," said their leader, turning about, "each one of you has his work to do, just as Henry has. See that you do it."

At once the boys returned to their posts, while Henry and his captain passed out of the house and went down the street. Instead of going directly to their destination, the two made their way by a roundabout route and kept a sharp lookout lest they should meet the grocer or his boy. But they passed almost no one and came soon to a little white house, not far from the grocer's store, that was set back in a yard behind a high hedge. Connected with the house was a small garage, built so as to resemble an extension of the dwelling.

A keen-eyed woman answered their knock at the door and looked at them questioningly.

"We are the sugar refiners sent by the Federal Sugar Company," said Captain Hardy, repeating the words given him by the secret service agent.

"I've been looking for you," replied the woman. "Come in." And she led them at once through the house to the garage.

Henry was about to ask Captain Hardy what he meant by saying that they were sugar refiners, but when he saw the motor-cycle that awaited him he forgot his question and gave a sharp cry of exultation. It was a beautiful machine, with tires so strong and thick they were practically puncture proof and were evidently equal to any demand that was likely to be made upon them. Evidently the engine was one of great power. The frame of the machine was a dark gray; and Henry instantly noted the fact that there was an almost utter absence of nickel about the motorcycle. The spokes, handle-bars, and trimmings were all enameled black. The headlight was a powerful electric one, with a black cap over the lens. With great interest Henry examined the spark- and gasoline-controls, the motor itself, and finally the muffler, which was of the most improved variety. He looked in the gasoline-tank and found it full. The oil-tank was brimming. Every moving part had been carefully greased and cleaned.

"What's this?" cried Henry, of a sudden, noting what seemed to be an extra and unnecessary piece of framework.

"Take it out and see," said Captain Hardy, with a smile.

Carefully Henry examined the fastenings, to see how the extra tubing was adjusted. Then he drew it forth.

"A metal cane," he said, puzzled. "What is it? What is it for?"

Captain Hardy explained. Then he picked up a small electric torch, some well insulated wires that lay coiled on a near-by chair, and something that looked like a giant fountain pen. He handed these articles to Henry, and repeated what the secret service man had told him as to their use.

"Put them in your pocket and be very careful that you do not lose them," directed Captain Hardy. "Carry them with you so that you can run to your motor-cycle at a second's notice. Now replace that cane on the machine."

Henry slid the cane back and fastened it in place. It was gray, like the car, and seemed to be a part of it. Then Captain Hardy fastened the little map case above the gasoline-tank in such a way that Henry could pluck out a map as he rode.

"Now," he said, "there is nothing to do but wait until the automobile driver comes for another dollar. Then you must follow him wherever he goes. You must watch every movement he makes. But you must not let him see you. It's a hard thing to ask of you, Henry, for everything hinges upon your success."

A look of determination flashed in Henry's eyes. "I'll do my best," he said simply.

"I know you will," rejoined his leader. Then he added, with a smile, "Now we'll go back to the eagle's nest and wait for the hawk to appear."

CHAPTER X

THE PURSUIT IN THE DARK

Day followed day but that bird of prey did not appear. "A watched pot never boils," said Henry at last, trying to conquer his impatience; and he turned his mind from the task of following the automobile driver to the even more difficult task of securing one of the dollars. For sooner or later the wireless patrol would have to procure one of these mysterious coins. But Henry could see no way to accomplish that end without alarming the quarry. Day after day the little patrol discussed the question. It was useless to think of securing a coin from the man on the cliff, from the grocer's boy, or from the grocer himself; for none of the three had possession of the coins very long after they were marked. And what became of the coins after they left the grocer's hands could as yet be only guessed at.

Again and again, as the days passed, the members of the wireless patrol discussed the secret of the dollars, but nowhere could they find even the suggestion of a solution. Slowly time dragged on. Day followed day. The watch grew monotonous and tiresome. There were no signs of hostile activity in the hawk's nest and the secret service had no suspicious telephone conversations to report. It required all their resolution to keep the young scouts at their task of

86   Lewis E. Theiss

listening in. They even began to think that they had been detected and that the activities of the spy in the hawk's nest were ended.

Then, one afternoon, galvanizing them to sudden action, came a cryptic message from the secret service, announcing that the Federal Sugar Company could use experienced refiners at once. Henry took the message, and recalling what Captain Hardy had told the woman when they went to see the motor-cycle, at once guessed its meaning. He ran to Captain Hardy and repeated it.

"You guessed rightly," said Captain Hardy. "Hereafter we, too, have to use code messages, and we just carried out the spy idea about sugar. This message is to warn us that transports are sailing. Go to your stations, boys."

Lew flew back to the wireless. Roy and Willie hustled down to the pine grove. Henry, his heart beating fast, hurried away to his motorcycle station.

For a long, long time nothing happened. Then a line of transports came into view. Presently the spy appeared at his window, sweeping the channel with his powerful glasses. For several moments he studied the passing ships carefully, then withdrew from the window and was lost to sight. In a very few moments the scouts saw the grocer's boy, with his basket and a few small packages, enter the house, then hurry away. Roy trailed him directly to the grocery store, but did not enter.

Henry, meantime, impatient, like Paul Revere, "to mount and ride," stood peering out of a tiny window of the garage, awaiting the expected motor-car. In his eagerness minutes seemed like hours. As time passed and no motorcar came, he began to believe that none would come, that the spies had learned of the trap set for them, and that they had discontinued their work or devised some new plan of operation. So impatient did Henry become that he could hardly refrain from running into the street to see if any motor-cars were approaching. At last his anxiety was relieved. He heard the regular beating of a motor climbing the hill. Then as he glued his eye to the tiny window the familiar car, a powerful roadster, with its top raised, rolled by. Again Henry tried to catch the number and failed. Then he knew that the dust-covered license number was not dust covered by accident. Quickly he noted the treads of the tires, and the shape of the wheel hubs, axles, and springs, so that he could identify the car. Then it passed from his sight.

And now his anxiety suddenly grew a hundredfold. Always before, the car had returned the way it came. Suppose that this time it should go back by another route and he should miss it. He could not endure the thought. Quickly he opened the door and peered forth. The driver was just turning his car, as he had always done before. The matter was settled. He would pass Henry's hiding place on his return. Quickly Henry shut the door and waited with what patience he could command.

For what seemed like an hour he waited. His pulse beat fast with excitement. He could hardly compel himself to stand quietly by his window and wait. The old fear that the motorist had gone away by some other route returned and began to torture him. He wanted to run out into the street and assure himself that the car was still in sight. And then, when it seemed he could endure the suspense not a second longer, he heard the purring of a motor, and the car he was waiting for slid quietly by and began to descend the hill toward the ferry.

At once a new fear sprang up in Henry's heart. Suppose the

Lewis E. Theiss

motor-cycle wouldn't go. Suppose he should be so slow as to miss the ferry-boat. Desperately he flung open the door and trundled his motor-cycle out to the street. The roadster was only a block ahead of him. Speedily Henry pushed the cycle along the road. The motor began to bark and Henry leaped to the saddle. In another instant he was speeding after the roadster and was already so near it that he had to jam on his brake to avoid coming up to it. Near the ferry there was more traffic and Henry felt relieved. He dropped back a little distance and was almost completely hidden from the roadster by the carts and cars between them. So they proceeded to the ferry, the suspected driver bringing his roadster to a halt near the front of the ferry-boat just as Henry, following a string of wagons and carts, reached the other end of the craft. Then the whistle blew and the boat pulled out into the Bay.

But Henry had now no eyes for the sights in the harbor that had formerly so fascinated him. His entire attention was centred on the roadster. The driver of the roadster remained in his seat, calmly looking out over the Bay. Henry stood his machine against a post and sought a position near by where he was sheltered from the spy's observation by a huge coal truck, but where he could himself distinctly see the roadster by peering through the spokes of the truck wheels. Again he made a mental inventory of the distinguishing features of the car he was following. And before the ferry-boat reached Manhattan he could have passed a perfect examination as to the appearance of the roadster.

It was already dusk when the boat slid into its slip, and the heavy clouds overhead gave promise of a dark night. Henry was thankful. Up Broadway he followed the roadster at a safe distance, then up Park Row, and so to the Brooklyn Bridge. Across this magic structure, one hundred and fifty feet above the surface of the water, Henry continued to follow the roadster. The great buildings, piled skyward in huge masses, were twinkling with a million lights. Boats were coming and going on the stream below. Electric cars followed one another across the bridge in endless procession. Elevated railway trains thundered past unceasingly. Upstream shone the fairy lights of the other bridges that span the East River. The Navy Yard lay in full view. But the scene that at other times Henry would have found entrancing, now he scarcely noticed. He had eyes for one thing only—the rolling motor-car ahead of him and the red eye that now glowed at its rear.

He turned on his light and at a safe distance followed the roadster, which was heading due east. They passed the business portions of Brooklyn. They left Prospect Park behind them. They traversed a region of apartment-houses. Then came less thickly settled districts, with block after block of private residences, each in its own little yard. And so they proceeded to the very outskirts of the city, where houses gave place to vacant lots and vacant lots were succeeded by open fields. Darkness had come. Traffic had grown less and less. Now there were no sheltering vehicles between himself and the roadster. A great fear of discovery sprang up in Henry's heart. He switched off his light, risking arrest, and rode on in the darkness. Occasionally he passed under a lone street lamp. And now he understood why his machine was enameled black instead of being nickel finished. It gave back no answering gleam when beams of light fell upon it. It was made for just the secret sort of work it was doing now. For, with his motor completely muffled, his lamp extinguished, Henry was now riding through the night like a dark shadow.

Long before this, Henry had slipped the proper map from its case and had followed his route as far as he was able to see. Though his eyes could no longer pierce the darkness, Henry knew that he was passing through a lonely, undeveloped

Lewis E. Theiss

section of land. Dimly he glimpsed tiny bits of woodland here and there. The lonely lights Henry occasionally saw were the lamps in isolated farmhouses. He could no longer tell exactly where he was, though he knew the road he was following. But he had watched his speedometer closely and he knew he was traveling about twenty miles an hour. He was keeping pace with the motor-car, but riding several hundred yards behind it. So they continued for a long time.

Suddenly the motor-car swung round a curve and vanished from sight. Henry knew the car had rounded a curve because he saw the lights swing. A minute later as he was about to reach the curve himself, he heard the rapid beating of hoofs and a team of horses came tearing round the bend and charged straight at him. Evidently the driver had lost control of them and it flashed into Henry's mind that they had been frightened by the roadster ahead. But he had no time to think of anything. The frantic animals bore down on him like an express-train. Quick as thought Henry turned sharply to the right and threw on his power. The horses were almost upon him. The driver glimpsed him, cursed him savagely for having no light, and gave a powerful heave on the reins. The horses swerved in one direction as Henry shot in the other, missing them by less than a foot. Before he could straighten his machine again, it had left the road and was plunging over the rough surface of a field.

Henry jammed his brake on so suddenly that it toppled him from the saddle, but neither he nor the machine was injured. He turned the motor-cycle about and headed for the road. And now his hair almost stood on end. In the darkness he could dimly see some great lumber piles, as large as houses. He had all but crashed into them at high speed. Now he understood why the roadster's light had disappeared when the car turned the curve. It had been hidden by these great lumber piles. Rapidly Henry ran back to the road. He knew the motor-car would now be far ahead of him. He should have to hasten to overtake it. He ran along the highway, pushing his machine, and leaped to the saddle when the engine began to explode regularly. Then he turned the curve and peered ahead into the darkness. The road seemed to lie straight before him, but the motor-car had utterly vanished.

For a moment Henry rode on, almost bewildered. Then he looked rapidly about him. No farmhouse was in sight to which the motorcar might have gone. No light gleamed anywhere. But he could dimly see trees here and there. And he made out a wooden fence lining the left side of the road.

"Lucky I didn't shoot in that direction when I met that team," muttered Henry. "I'd have gone clear through that fence." He dismounted, set his machine up, and took out his pocket torch. Holding it close to the road, he began to examine the highway. "There are the marks of his rear tires," he muttered.

And thankful indeed was the puzzled scout that he had learned so well at Camp Brady to observe carefully. He mounted his wheel and rode a few hundred yards further. Then he examined the road again. He found the tracks he was searching for. He rode on and dismounting, found in two places the telltale marks. But the third time he examined the highway there were no marks of the roadster's tires visible.

"He left the road between this point and the last stop," murmured Henry.

He went back a hundred feet and searched. There were no tire marks. Another hundred feet showed no prints in the dust. But the third hundred revealed the wheel marks. "Ah!" said Henry, "he turned off close by."

He set his wheel against the fence and went forward,

following the prints with his light, which he shaded carefully and held close to the road. Within fifty feet the marks turned straight off to the left. The car had passed from the highway through a gap in the fence, into an open field. What the field was like Henry could only conjecture. He dared not flash his light around to see.

He ran back and got his machine, then followed the wheel prints into the field. They did not show readily on the grassy surface, and soon he had lost them altogether. At first a sense of fear clutched at his heart. He recalled his leader's words as to the dangerous nature of this duty. Here he was in exactly the lonely situation his captain had foreseen, by himself, and with no means of defense. The enemy he was trailing had disappeared. He might be a mile distant or he might be waiting for his pursuer, behind the nearest tree. Henry shivered with fear and stood irresolute. But the feeling passed when he realized that he had lost the trail, that his quarry had escaped him, that he had failed his captain. A wave of remorse swept over him. The sense of fear left him entirely, and he bent all his energies to the task of finding the motor-car. He hid his wheel in a thicket that he might work faster, pausing only to snatch from it the metal cane fastened to the frame.

Cautiously he glided forward, crouching as he moved, and taking advantage of every rock and bush he could see to screen himself. He held his breath and listened. Now he crept forward a foot at a time. Now he advanced swiftly for yards. He worked his way to the right and the left. But nowhere could he see what he was searching for, and no betraying sound came out of the thick blackness.

"It's no use," he said to himself bitterly, after he had searched for a quarter of an hour. "I have lost him, and if I am not careful I'll lose his message as well."

Near by he could dimly discern a tall stump. He ran over to it and on it laid his map, a pencil, his electric torch, his knife, the wires that he had been carrying in his pocket, and the giant fountain pen. Grasping the tip of his cane he gave a sharp tug and an inner lining slid outward. From this he drew out a third length, and from that a fourth. His metal cane was in reality an extension rod, not unlike a telescoping fishing-rod. It was fully ten feet long. In its curved handle was a small opening, like a keyhole. Into this Henry jammed the bayonet connection that terminated one of the wires. The other end of the wire he thrust into a like opening in the side of his big fountain pen. Into the opposite side of his pen he fastened one end of his second wire, attaching the other end of this wire to his knife, which he thrust deep into the earth. Then, raising the extended cane aloft with his left hand, he put the point of his fountain pen to his right ear and listened. The mysterious articles that the secret service had supplied constituted a complete wireless receiving set. He could catch any message sent from a point within six or eight miles.

He was not a moment too soon. Hardly had he gotten the fountain pen adjusted before there came a crackling in his ear. He rested his cane, upright, against the stump, and began to tune his instrument by sliding the cap of the fountain pen in and out. In a second he had tuned it perfectly. The sounds came to him with startling clearness.

"He's near at hand," muttered Henry.

He seized his pencil and wrote down on his map the letters that were sounding in his ear. Then with frantic haste he disconnected his instrument, telescoped his extension cane, and gathered up the different articles and thrust them into his pockets. As rapidly as he could pick his way, he went back to his hidden machine. He fastened the metal cane in place, and got everything ready for a quick start.

Lewis E. Theiss

Suddenly a faint purring noise came to his ears. "Ah!" muttered Henry, "he's started his motor. He's off in that direction. What shall I do?"

His first impulse was to run at speed toward the purring motor, and to try to locate exactly the position of the hidden wireless station. But discretion showed him that was not wise. The spy might turn his lights on at any moment and Henry would be caught. Then everything was lost.

"I must make sure I can find the place in the daytime," muttered Henry. Carefully he gauged the sound, deciding whence it came. "He's right off there," he said. And with his heel he made a long mark in the turf, pointing straight toward the sound.

Almost before he finished, the sound grew louder and Henry knew the car was advancing. He shrank back into the thicket, dragging his motor-cycle with him. An instant later the roadster rolled softly past, not more than fifty feet distant. In a moment more the car had reached the fence and turned into the highway. Its lights suddenly flashed out and the car went bowling down the road toward Brooklyn.

Henry leaped from the thicket and ran toward the highway, pushing his motor-cycle before him. He paused at the opening in the fence, and with his knife smoothed a space on one of the posts and marked a cross on it with his pencil. Then he ran to the highway, started his motor, and was soon flying down the road in pursuit of the roadster. And as he had come, so he returned, with lights out, until Brooklyn was reached and the streets were once more alive with traffic.

At a safe distance he followed the unsuspecting motorist and saw him turn into a private yard in Flatbush. Instantly Henry dismounted, thrust his wheel behind a hedge that fenced a private residence, and gained a position where he could watch the spy's house. He saw the spy close and lock his garage and enter the house. Stealthily Henry approached and noted the house number. At the corner he got the name of the street. Then he hurried back to his hidden motor-cycle and was soon flying back to his comrades at the eagle's nest.

Lewis E. Theiss

CHAPTER XI

AN UNSUCCESSFUL SEARCH

It was characteristic of Henry that he should tell the worst about himself first. In his own manly way he was willing to accept the blame for his failure.

"He got away from me," he began, so chagrined that he could hardly repress the tears. "I didn't find the hidden wireless and I have failed in my task."

Before his captain he stood with downcast eyes and tortured heart. His experience at Camp Brady had taught him that the wireless patrol expected every member to do his duty—and he had failed.

Captain Hardy looked at his lieutenant for a moment without answering. He had not the slightest idea of what had occurred, but he recognized instantly the manliness of Henry's report. The latter was offering no excuses, making no attempt to shield himself from the consequences of his failure.

"Suppose you tell us just what happened," said the leader gently, "and we can judge better how badly you have failed."

Gratefully Henry looked up. He had not expected a scolding. That was not Captain Hardy's way of disciplining his boys. But he had felt sure his leader would show how deeply he was disappointed, for Captain Hardy was terribly in earnest in this quest for spies. So once again Henry's heart went out to his captain. Rapidly he related what had befallen him. As he proceeded with his story, his leader's face lost its look of grave concern, his eyes began to flash with interest, his cheeks to burn with eagerness. When Henry's narrative had reached the point where the motor-car had disappeared in the field and Henry was searching for it. Captain Hardy held up his hand.

"Stop a moment," he interrupted. "You were in no wise to blame for what happened, and instead of being condemned for failure you are to be commended for your success. Many a boy would never have found where that car went. And even though you did not learn exactly where the car was, you have located the field and you may be sure that driver never went very far in a field. We shall find the place easily enough. Go on."

Henry looked at his leader gratefully and a happy light came into his eyes. "Do you really think I didn't fail?" he asked eagerly.

"Assuredly," insisted Captain Hardy. "I think that you have learned enough to enable us to locate this hidden station. Go on."

Henry proceeded with the story of his search in the dark, of his uncertainty as to what he should do, of his fear of missing the message as well as the car, and of how he had intercepted that message, marked the fence post, and located the home of the automobile driver.

Lewis E. Theiss

"Why, Henry," cried Captain Hardy, when the recital was ended, "whatever put it into your head that you had failed? You have done well—exceedingly well."

"But I didn't find the hidden station, and you said that was so important."

"That is a mere detail, Henry. We shall find it easily enough. We have our experience at Elk City to direct us."

"That's just why I felt so bad," said Henry. "If these Germans have concealed their wireless plant as skilfully as the dynamiters did at Elk City, we may never find where it is."

"We'll try before we give up hope," said the captain smiling. "And even if we never find it, we now know something more important than the location of one of their several wireless plants. We know where another member of the gang lives. That is excellent, Henry, excellent! The Chief will be more than pleased. I know he is a great deal more concerned about this wireless situation than he permits us to think. The public is clamoring for protection for the troops and the Chief simply cannot accomplish one-fourth of what is demanded of him. If we uncover this gang for him, we shall do a very real service to America, boys."

"We'll do it," cried Willie vehemently. "We'll do it. We'll get 'em just as sure as we got the dynamiters."

"I believe we shall," smiled the captain. "And if that's the way you all feel about it, I know we shall. We're closing in on them fast. To-morrow we'll go out to that field Henry has marked and see what we can find in the daylight."

So it happened that the succeeding forenoon found the five members of the wireless patrol rolling rapidly toward the point of investigation, in a motor-car furnished by the secret service and driven by one of its agents. Henry sat beside the driver and pointed out the way, while the others crowded into the rear of the car.

With his map on his knees Henry traced the way. Speedily they passed through the built-up portion of Brooklyn and came shortly to the sparsely settled district through which their road ran. Henry scanned the way with curious interest. He had been over the road but he knew nothing of what he had passed. Occasionally they whirled by a tree close to the road that Henry thought he had glimpsed in the darkness. So they flew forward until Henry, looking eagerly ahead, cried out, "There are the lumber piles."

The driver slowed his car almost to a walk and they looked in the dust for telltale marks. Few teams had passed since Henry's adventure, and in the dust could still plainly be seen the marks of Henry's wheel as he had turned sharply into the field, and the narrow tracks of the vehicle that had almost run him down.

But Henry was more interested in marks of another sort. "There!" he cried suddenly. "See those tracks? They're the marks of the spy's roadster." And he pointed to parallel tread marks, one made by a chain tread tire and one by a diamond tread.

They passed on. Not many hundred yards distant was an opening in the fence. "That's the place he turned off," insisted Henry. "See that light place where I shaved the post?"

But they did not turn into the field. Instead the motor-car continued steadily on its way. A half mile up the highway was a road-house known to the driver.

"It's about eleven o'clock now," said the secret service man. "We'll have luncheon at the roadhouse and in the meantime we can stroll around and hunt up this wireless plant. We'd attract too much attention if we drove directly into the field."

They stopped at the road-house, ordered luncheon, and said they would stroll about until noon. Then they wandered, apparently aimlessly, about the place and into the fields. The country was nearly level, with slight depressions here and little hillocks there, and bits of woodland all about. The road-house was the only structure in sight, and when they had passed beyond a slight elevation, even this was hidden. Apparently there was not a soul in the neighborhood. They paused just inside a little grove and made sure that no one was following them from the road-house. Then they pushed rapidly on into the little thicket which Henry recognized as his hiding-place of the previous night.

After a moment's search, Henry found the mark he had made in the turf. "The motor-car was in that direction," he explained, pointing along his turf mark.

His fellows looked in the direction of his outstretched arm. At a distance of a quarter of a mile was a thick little grove. Henry was pointing straight at the heart of it.

The scouts had kept themselves well hidden in the thicket as Henry was finding his mark. If any one was in the wood, that person could not as yet see them.

"I have no doubt we shall find the secret station in that grove," said Captain Hardy. "I see several tall trees sticking up above the others that might conceal aerials. I doubt if any one is there now, but some one might be. So we shall have to approach carefully and in such a way that we can capture any one who might be within the grove. Suppose we advance on it from all four sides, as we did on the willow copse at the Elk City reservoir. Then if any one is within the grove we shall see him."

The leader gave each boy his orders and the advance began. Henry was to circle and enter the woods from the rear. Roy was to approach from one side and Willie from the other. Lew was to go in at the front. Captain Hardy and the secret service man were to station themselves outside the wood so that they could see every point of its exterior and detect any one leaving it. Each glided away toward his post.

At a given signal from Captain Hardy, the boys began to work their way silently from their posts into the grove. This was small in extent and such precautions seemed almost unnecessary. But after their desperate experience with the dynamiters, the members of the wireless patrol were taking no chances. They knew full well that discretion is the better part of valor. And they knew, in addition, that the success of their search might depend upon the caution with which they proceeded. So they went forward, when the captain's signal rang out, like so many Indians on the war-path, stalking a hated enemy.

Indeed they were almost as invisible as Indians. Each had circled skilfully to his post. And now each crept forward silently, slipping from rock to bush, taking advantage of the slightest cover, and advancing so stealthily through the tall grass that even the two men on watch outside the grove could hardly tell where the scouts were moving. And any one inside the grove could not have detected them at all.

The four scouts reached the four sides of the grove almost simultaneously. Each of the four crept round the trunk of a big tree and squatted down with the trunk at his back, to look and to listen. From side to side their eyes roved, examining every tree and stump in sight. But they saw nothing on the ground or in the branches overhead to alarm them. There was no indication of human presence other than their own; and Willie was certain that the wood was deserted, for several small flocks of birds flew up in alarm as he penetrated the grove. Had other men been within the wood, he knew the birds would long ago have been frightened away.

Slowly the four scouts worked their way toward the centre of the grove, gliding round the trunks of trees and stopping every few feet to look and listen. But they heard nothing, saw nothing, to indicate that any man was within the grove. Each one, as he advanced, scouted to right and left of his line of march, so that when the four met in the centre of the wood, they had covered every rod of ground within the grove. And they had found nobody.

What was more, they had seen no signs of a wireless outfit. But, in view of their experience in searching for the dynamiters' hidden wireless, this was not surprising. None of the scouts had expected to find the secret plant without a thorough search. As soon as Captain Hardy and the secret service man joined them, a systematic search of the wood was begun.

There could not have been more than two hundred trees in the little grove. Satisfied that the place contained no enemy agents, Captain Hardy took his company to one end of the ground and began a careful examination of each tree. The six searchers strung out in a line across the grove, testing each tree as they advanced. They scanned the trunks and thumped them with clubs to make sure that they were not hollow. They peered at them from all sides, looking for holes and hollow limbs. With sticks they scratched away the leaves from about the bases of the trees, turning up the soil for several inches and testing it for hidden wires. All the trees seemed sound. No hollow limbs were discovered. No suspicious marks were found in the earth about the tree trunks. The tall trees noted by Captain Hardy seemed never to have been touched by man. From tree to tree the search proceeded until every tree in the grove had been tested and the scouts were on the far edge of the wood. But no hidden wire, no secret instruments, no skilfully concealed aerials were found.

Blankly the searchers looked at one another. "It must be here," said Henry. "I am absolutely certain that the motor-car came from this direction and was about this distance from where I stood. And the signals were so loud and clear that I'm just sure they were sent from some spot close by."

"Let us look for wheel tracks," suggested Captain Hardy. "If we can find where the car stopped, we shall know that the message was sent from some point near by. Search along the sides of the grove first."

The party divided, and three searchers examined the ground along each side of the grove. Walking abreast and several feet distant from one another, they covered a broad strip of ground. Twice each party retraced its tracks but found nothing.

"Try another strip, farther away from the grove," said Captain Hardy.

Again the searchers lined up and went slowly forward on either side of the woods. Bending low, stepping slowly, sometimes kneeling to examine a suspicious mark, they moved carefully on. The thick turf had taken no telltale imprint.

"I fear it's useless," sighed the leader.

"Let's try again," pleaded Willie. "The car was here. We know that. And somewhere it was bound to make a mark. It might have gone beyond the grove."

They made another search, this time extending their examination to the land beyond the wood. Suddenly Roy gave a cry. "Here it is," he called.

The others ran to him. And there, sure enough, in a little bare spot between two hummocks of grass, was the plain imprint of a diamond tread. Instantly Roy and Willie dropped to their knees and began to feel along the line of the tire mark.

Henry and Lew, meantime, searched to right and left of them. "Here's his other wheel track," suddenly cried Lew, and there, sure enough, was a distinct impression of a chain tread tire.

They proceeded in the direction in which the car had been moving. "Here's where he turned," cried Henry.

The turf before him was torn and ragged. Distinctly they could see the impression made by the driving wheels as they gripped the ground in starting.

"Then here is where he stood," said Captain Hardy. "It is immediately behind the wood. Your mark pointed straight enough, Henry, but your man was farther away than you thought. Probably he ran behind this grove to make doubly sure he would not be seen from the highway. The hidden station must be in this end of the grove. We'll search again."

Once more they plunged into the wood. Again they examined every tree. Up one trunk after another shinned Roy and Lew, who were born climbers. But hunt as they would, search as they might, they found nothing to indicate a secret wireless. At last, completely baffled, they gave up the search.

"It's here," insisted Captain Hardy. "Our experience at the Elk City reservoir makes me sure of that. They're too clever for us. But we'll get them yet. We'll follow that roadster so closely next time that we can't miss the secret. It's too bad, boys, but don't be discouraged. We have done much to come so close. Now we'll go back to the road-house. It's long past time for luncheon."

CHAPTER XII

ANOTHER OBSTACLE

Time wore on. Now that there was something definite to work on, the secret service began to take a more active part in the spy hunt.

"You have helped us greatly," said the Chief to Captain Hardy, one day. "My men were so rushed with work that they simply could not take the time to go hunting round for clues. But now that the wireless patrol has furnished those clues, we shall be able to follow them up. But we want you to continue at work just the same. You can still help us."

But the members of the wireless patrol, and especially Henry, found small satisfaction in the Chief's praise. They had not come to New York merely to furnish the secret service with clues. They had come to uncover the system by which spies were betraying the movements of our transports. At the Elk City reservoir they had succeeded where trained men had failed; and they meant to succeed here also. They felt that the Chief was patting them on the head, as it were, and telling them that they were good little boys. They meant to show him they were the equals of his own men, even if the Chief's words, instead of pleasing them, stimulated them to half angry activity.

"He needn't think that just because we're boys and come from the country we aren't any good," argued Roy. "That's the way everybody talks about boys. That's the way they talked about us at Elk City until we caught the dynamiters and showed them what we could do. We'll show Uncle Sam's men, too. I don't care if they are famous detectives. We'll get these fellows ourselves. We're not going to have the secret service step in now and take all the credit."

But it was one thing to talk so confidently and quite another to accomplish the end they were striving for. They had not yet discovered a single one of the hidden wireless stations, and the secret of the dollar was still a secret. As far as the members of the wireless patrol could see, it was likely to remain a secret. How they could secure one of the dollars without being detected, they did not know; and how they were to read the message, even if they did get the dollar, was more than they could see; for by this time they had dropped the idea that the messages were engraved on the coins. More and more those dollars appeared a great and insuperable obstacle.

"Couldn't we manage to see the spy when he marks those dollars?" asked Roy. "Is there any way that we could get into his house and hide, so as to watch him?"

"You mustn't think of trying," said Captain Hardy decisively. "But possibly you could find a new place to watch from that would enable you to see him better. These field-glasses of mine are very powerful, and if you can find the proper view-point, you can see him well, even from a distance."

Without a word Roy grabbed his hat and darted out of the house. A second later he was slipping through the thicket on the sloping hillside. Cautiously he crawled from one point to another. The only station that gave any promise of success

Lewis E. Theiss

was the pine grove originally selected. The tree from which they had been watching the spy's house was a giant pine that towered above every other tree in the grove. But the scouts had never dared to ascend beyond the protecting foliage of the other trees, lest they be detected. So they had been looking upward at an angle, as they watched the spy's house. Roy now saw that if he were to climb high up in the big pine, he would be on a level with the spy's windows, and could doubtless see clearly into the house. The difficulty would be to make the climb without being detected.

Roy made his way back to headquarters and reported on his observations. "I didn't go up," he said, "for fear he would see me."

"You were wise," replied Captain Hardy. "We must devise some plan by which you can get up the tree unnoticed."

"Camouflage!" said Willie suddenly. "Fix one of us up like a pine tree. Then he won't see us."

"Just the idea," said Lew laughing.

"We'll have to use the smallest boy in the bunch," said Captain Hardy, "and that's you, Willie. Come. We'll see what we can do with you. Go get me some samples of pine bark and needles."

Willie speedily got the desired objects. Captain Hardy examined them critically. "You ought to have a dark brown suit, painted with irregular stripes, like branches, and dabs of green, like foliage."

"Don't forget his face," cried Roy in glee. "That will have to be painted brown and green also."

A laugh went up. "I'm merely telling what ought to be done, Willie," said Captain Hardy reassuringly, "not what we shall do. We have to guard against observation by persons other than this spy. If the neighbors saw a boy going out of here garbed the way you want Willie fixed up, Roy, they would begin to ask questions. And we don't know what the spy's relations are with his neighbors. What we shall have to do is to dress Willie in clothes as nearly the color of the tree as possible. We can get shoes, stockings, and a suit of clothes to match the tree trunk. We can get a cap the shade of these pine-needles. That leaves hands and face. They, too, must be disguised. A pair of gloves of the proper shade will take care of the hands. But what about the face?"

"Nothing for it but to paint it," said Roy, his eyes dancing.

"I guess you're right," said Captain Hardy. Willie made a wry face. The captain saw him. "The trench raiders blacken both their hands and faces when they steal out into No Man's Land at night," he said. "But we won't use real paint, Willie. We'll get some theatrical paint that comes off easily. I'll get the necessary materials at once."

He noted down the sizes needed and went out. And it was well he acted so promptly. That very afternoon a message from the secret service informed them that more transports were sailing.

"Come with me and get on your pine tree outfit, Willie," suggested their leader. "You other boys go to your stations at once."

Henry's task henceforth was to trail the driver of the roadster. He hurried away to his waiting motor-cycle. Lew was at the wireless key again. Roy scurried out to the pine grove, and Willie followed his captain to be "camouflaged." A few moments later, dressed in his new brown clothes, and a chocolate brown in complexion, he slipped from the house and joined Roy.

Impatiently they waited for the first transport to appear. It was a long time coming. But finally Willie picked it out with his glasses, far up the Bay, as it nosed its way steadily through the rolling waves. Behind it was another transport. As the ships drew near, Willie mounted as far up in the tree as he dared, crouching behind the tops of the surrounding trees, and hugging his own tree trunk, motionless, awaiting his opportunity to climb to his ultimate post. His heart beat fast. His legs shook slightly with excitement. He was trembling all over, so eager was he to make the ascent. On came the boats. Long ago they had passed Robbin's Reef. Now they were well into the Narrows. Suddenly the spy appeared at his window, sweeping the channel with his glasses, his hands shutting off his vision on the sides, like blinders on a horse. Quickly Willie scurried up the tree, wrapping himself closely about the slender trunk, concealing as much of his body as he could, and snuggling behind the sparse clumps of foliage. Then he brought his glasses to bear, and sat silently studying the spy's house.

The interior of the dwelling was as he had guessed it to be. There was no partition wall in the forward part of the building, a single column upholding the ceiling, so that, above the low sash curtains, Willie could see entirely through the glassed-in room. This was more than comfortable. Willie saw a row of low book-shelves lining the north side of the great room. There were numerous fine pictures and plaster casts here and there. A piano stood in one corner, a talking-machine in another. The light within seemed to flicker, and Willie guessed that in the rear of the room, where he could not see it, a log was burning in an open fireplace; for the days were growing very chilly.

But before Willie could complete his observations, the spy turned from the window and walked toward a large, flat desk in the centre of the room. Willie shrank close against the tree and remained as motionless as a stone image. But the spy never once glanced out of the window. He sank into a chair before the desk, switched on an electric desk light, and began to write on a piece of paper. Evidently he was arranging his message. When this was done to his satisfaction, he reached into the desk and drew forth a dollar. Willie could see it plainly as the spy laid it on his desk blotter, under the lamp. Intently Willie strained forward. The spy leaned forward and fumbled about the bottom of his desk. His hands and arms were hidden and Willie could only conjecture what was happening. Then Willie gave a little gasp of surprise as the spy straightened up and laid on the blotter beside the dollar a curious little thing like nothing Willie had ever seen. Evidently it was of metal for it shone under the light. Willie screwed up his face as he strained his eyes to identify the object. It seemed to be a disc of exactly the same size as the dollar. Yet it was not solid, because Willie could see the blotter through it. To Willie the thing resembled nothing so much as a spider-web. What it was, Willie could not even guess.

Meantime the spy had pulled open a drawer, from which he took a slender instrument, which also Willie could not identify. But evidently it had a sharp point; for the spy, after placing the disc on the dollar, scratched the milled edge of the coin with the little instrument, then he began to make marks here and there through the little disc, on the surface of the dollar. From time to time he turned the coin, and occasionally he looked at the writing on his paper. He seemed quite expert, for he worked fast. He finished his task and leaned over behind his desk, evidently to put the curious disc in its secret repository.

Lewis E. Theiss

Quick as a flash, Willie slid from his exposed perch and safely gained the concealing shelter of the lower tree tops before the spy straightened up again. Willie climbed on down the tree and joined Roy at the usual observation post.

"What did you see?" asked Roy eagerly.

When Willie had told him, Roy groaned. "Gee! That makes it all the harder. Now we've got to get one of those discs as well as a marked dollar before we can discover how they send their messages."

The grocer's boy came and went. Roy trailed him back to the store, but prudently kept out of sight. There was nothing to be gained by entering the store again. Meantime Willie scrambled up to the house and related to Lew and his captain what he had seen. And they agreed with Roy that the problem, instead of being easier, had become more difficult.

CHAPTER XIII

WHAT HENRY DISCOVERED

Henry, meantime, was waiting at his station with eagerness and quickened determination. Despite his leader's generous words, Henry felt in his heart that his last effort had been a failure. It was true that he had made it possible to learn the identity of the driver of the roadster, and that the secret service men had in the meanwhile been looking up the man's record; but Henry felt that he should also have discovered the location of the secret wireless. Now he made up his mind that nothing should balk him in the present attempt. That neither accident nor anything else should hinder him from accomplishing his purpose. He would be more skilful than he had ever been before. He would watch closer. He would follow his quarry, as silently as a shadow and as closely. He would do all that his leader expected of him—and more.

Thus resolving, steeling his mind to the greatest effort of his life, Henry stood at the little window in the garage, all atremble with eagerness. He thought he knew every inch of the spy's roadster, but when that car finally rolled past, Henry studied it as he had never studied anything before. Again he noted the tread of each tire and looked for cuts or other distinguishing marks in them. As good luck would have it, a turning wagon obstructed the roadster just as it

Lewis E. Theiss

reached the little garage, and the roadster came almost to a dead stop. Henry studied its running-gear, its radiator and bonnet, its dash-board and wind-shield. And when his eyes got so far, they went no further. The standards that held up the wind-shield were bulkier and thicker than any other such parts Henry could remember. The difference was not great, yet there was a difference; and like the accomplished scout he was, Henry noted that difference and questioned it. But, like Willie with the spider-web disc, he was completely puzzled. The enlarged standards might mean anything or nothing. The car rolled on and again Henry looked in vain at the number. Some part of it was always dust covered. But Henry observed that the hidden figures were not the same from day to day.

When the car returned from the grocer's, Henry jumped to his motor-cycle and made his way to the ferry by a route different from the roadster's. He knew he was taking a chance, but he also knew that an accomplice might be trailing the roadster to see if the latter were watched. Henry could follow the spy to the ferry once without arousing much suspicion; but if he were twice seen to do so, his usefulness might be ended. He knew when the ferry-boat would leave its slip and he made his way aboard just before the gate closed.

At once he had a feeling that he had acted wisely. The roadster was again in the forward part of the boat, but this time the driver did not sit placidly looking out over the Bay. He seemed nervous, and every little while turned sharp around and looked about him. Fortunately Henry had concealed his wheel behind a truck and was himself where the spy could not see him. When he noted the spy's restlessness, it flashed into his mind that perhaps the secret service men who had been investigating this spy had not been so careful as they should have been, and that the spy had taken alarm. It was a discouraging thought, for it made Henry's task vastly more difficult. Wisely, therefore, he went into the cabin and sat down. The spy could not see him, and if the latter should stroll about the boat, there was nothing to indicate to whom the motor-cycle belonged.

As the gate opened and the roadster rolled from the ferry-boat, Henry prudently remained well behind it. Up Broadway they went, as fast as the traffic would allow, their pace gradually quickening as they drew away from the congested lower end of the island. The spy drove straight up Broadway. He circled Union Square and continued north. He passed Madison Square and still held to Broadway. Past the shopping district, past Longacre Square, past Columbus Circle, the roadster continued, still on the city's main highway. And at a discreet distance Henry followed.

Now they reached the apartment-house district and slid past block after block of bulky living apartments. And so they continued past Columbia University and down the grade beyond. And here Henry's troubles began. The roadster turned to the left, and Henry knew the driver was making for the Fort Lee ferry.

How should he gain the boat unnoticed? How should he follow, undetected, along the Jersey roads? For after they had crossed the Hudson there would be an end to that concealing traffic that had so far hidden him. He must follow the roadster over lonely roads and yet remain unseen. It was a problem to disturb any one. And it worried Henry not a little. Fortunately dusk was at hand, though the curtaining darkness would not fall for some time.

When the boat reached the Jersey shore, Henry permitted the roadster to get a long start before he went ashore. The spy turned to the right and began to climb the long grade parallel to the river, that would lead him to the top of the Palisades. When the roadster was almost out of sight, Henry mounted his motor-cycle and followed. Even if his quarry should pass completely from view, Henry had no fear of losing him; for the roadster's tracks were plain in the dusty road.

The dusk deepened. As it grew darker, Henry came closer to his quarry, though he kept behind elevations and curves in the road so as still to remain invisible to the driver of the car ahead. Thus they rode for some miles. The country was as Henry had pictured it from his study of the maps. It was sparsely built up, woodlands were on every hand, and the surface of the land was rolling and rock-strewn. It was an excellent place in which to hide—and also an excellent place in which to dodge one's enemies. As Henry thought of this, he drew closer and closer to the car, though still seeking to remain out of sight. As the light failed, and it became difficult to distinguish the marks in the dust before him, Henry drew up so that he could see the roadster, but he discreetly rode close to the side of the highway, where the overhanging trees shadowed him. Even had the roadster's driver been looking straight in his direction, he might never have seen Henry. He was, as he had determined to be, a veritable shadow.

So they rolled northward. At last it grew dark. The driver of the roadster switched on his lights. Now Henry crept still closer. He was in the dark, his lamp unlighted, his motor running silently, and he had no further fear of discovery.

It was well that darkness had come. They had now reached a lonely region where there were few houses. Here, Henry judged, was an excellent place for a secret wireless. And he judged correctly, for hardly had the thought come into his mind before the roadster turned sharply to the left and disappeared. Henry darted up the road. He came at once to what he judged was a large field. Trees no longer bordered the highway on the left side. Dimly Henry saw objects here and there which he thought were boulders and clumps of bushes. He saw no light and stood for a second peering into the darkness, listening with bated breath. Straight ahead of him he heard the faint purring of a muffled motor. He knew that he was not many hundred feet behind it and that this time the car could not escape him. He thrust his motor-cycle into some near-by bushes, first whipping out his metal cane. Then he ran speedily but carefully after the car.

Evidently it was moving cautiously. Henry rapidly drew near to it. When he had come so close that he could see it distinctly, he dropped to a walk and began to look about, trying to see what was around him. Here in the field it was lighter than it had been on the highway under the shadowing trees. The field was, as Henry had guessed, a piece of wild land, grown up with thickets, with great boulders here and there. Directly ahead of him was a clump of bushes. Henry hastened to put them between himself and the car. It was well he did; for hardly had he gotten behind them before the car stopped and the driver got out. The car was not more than two hundred feet distant.

Henry dropped to the ground and lay still for a moment. Then he crept, like an Indian, toward the sheltering thicket. Through it he advanced until he was not more than fifty feet from the motor-car. He could see with fair distinctness, but was himself completely concealed. He lay like a log, watching intently.

The driver unfastened his top and slid it backward. As he did so, his overcoat caught on the open door and he gave an exclamation of impatience. When he had laid his top back, he lowered the upper half of his wind-shield. Then, standing on the running-board, he tugged at the top of his wind-shield standard. Up came a sliding inner tube. In a flash the entire mystery stood revealed to Henry. The wind-shield standard contained a collapsible mast, like the telescoping cane he held in his hand. Doubtless an aerial was now fastened to the mast. Somewhere within the car was a wireless outfit. Instead of having many secret stations, the Germans had this one portable station.

"How clever!" thought Henry. "And how well they deceived us."

The spy proceeded to run up his mast. It must have reached twenty feet into the air. And the aerial was dangling from it, too. Evidently the spy had fastened that on before raising the mast. Fifty feet distant stood a tree. The spy took something from the baggage container and walked over to the tree, where, Henry judged by the sound, he was fastening a hook. Then the spy carried over the other end of his aerial and fastened it to the hook. In the darkness Henry could see nothing of the details of this outfit, but he realized that the spy now had an aerial at least fifty feet long and well above the ground. For short distance communication it would answer perfectly.

The spy returned to his car and got into the seat beside the driver's. Henry wormed his way forward as far as he dared, hardly breathing, fascinated by what he beheld. For now he could see plainly. The spy had turned on a tiny light on his dashboard. Cautiously Henry rose to his feet, keeping behind a thick bush, and peered over the side of the car. The spy took a key from his pocket and unfastened a hidden lock. The entire cowl board turned down, revealing a compact but powerful wireless outfit. The aerial wire evidently was strung up within the collapsing mast.

From within the cowl the spy drew forth a curious metal

disc, not unlike a spider-web, and like nothing Henry had ever seen. He did not know what it was. He hardly breathed as he stood watching. Then the spy took a dollar from his pocket, examined the milled edge until he found a scratch, fitted the curious disc over the dollar, and turning the coin in his hand, slowly began to make letters on a slip of paper on the inverted dash. When he had finished writing, he fastened the disc back in the cowl, dropped the dollar in his overcoat pocket, and began to send the message he had deciphered from the dollar.

Henry leaned forward. He had no need of his own receiving instrument to catch the letters. And he could not have used it if he had needed it. But it was not important that he should catch the message. The powerful sparks that were leaping across the spy's spark-gap told him that a battery of considerable force was being used, and he knew that Lew would catch that message away back on Staten Island. Lew had caught the preceding message from Long Island, and it had been sent from a distance fully as great as this. With distinctness the letters came to Henry's ears and he realized that the man before him was an expert operator. But the letters he heard made no sense. They would have to be deciphered before the message could be understood.

However, it was not the message that Henry was thinking of. It was the dollar in the man's overcoat. "How could he get it? How could he get it?" he asked himself over and over. A hundred wild ideas flashed through his head, but he could think of no way to secure the coin without betraying himself.

Even as he was considering the matter, the spy finished sending his message and snapped off his light. Tiny as the illumination had been, the man was apparently completely blinded by the sudden darkness. As he stepped from his seat, his overcoat again caught on the swinging door. With an impatient oath he tore the coat from him and flung it on the running-board. Then he felt for his tools and walked over to the tree to lower the far end of his aerial.

Henry's chance had come. With a bound he was beside the car. Crouching, he seized the huddled coat, ran his hands tremblingly over it, located the pocket, found the dollar, dropped the coat where he had gotten it, and slipped back to his cover.

He was not a second too soon. In his eagerness to get the coin he had been clumsy, and had fumbled excitedly for several seconds before he found it. Meantime, the spy, with practised skill, had taken down both wires and fastening, and was well on his way back to the car. But Henry gained his cover and was safe.

A sudden fear smote him lest he betray himself. His heart beat so loudly he was sure the spy would hear it. His breath came so excitedly he was certain he could be heard yards away. For some time he crouched motionless, hugging the ground, trying to hold his breath. But as second followed second and the spy made no outcry, Henry gained confidence. Suddenly a feeling of exultation came to him, so strong that he could hardly refrain from shouting. For the first time he thought of the real significance of what he had accomplished. He had unraveled the mystery of the wireless. He had the dollar. The secrets the wireless patrol had worked so hard to uncover were within his grasp. As the full meaning of it all came to him, he felt that he must cry out, that he must give voice to his feelings. He no longer dared trust himself to remain where he was, lest he betray himself. Clutching the dollar as he had never clung to anything in his life, he picked up his cane and slowly began to worm his way backward, on his belly, from the thicket. With the utmost caution, an inch at a time, he moved, lest he snap a stick or strike a stone with his foot. As soon as he was clear of the brush, he faced about, and crawled into the darkness.

The spy, meantime, was proceeding rapidly in reassembling his car. Henry heard the windshield go up and the top being fastened. He heard the baggage lid snap into place. Then he heard the spy swearing in a low voice. Henry stopped, still as a hunted rabbit.

"*Donnerwetter!*" he heard the man say. "I've lost that dollar." There was a pause. Then came the words, "I'm not going to hunt for it anyway. Somebody would see my light sure. And if anybody does find it, he'll never guess what it is."

Exultantly Henry rose to his feet, and crouching low, ran with soft, swift tread to his motorcycle. He had the dollar. The owner believed it was lost. Never was such luck. Trembling all over, he fastened his cane to the frame of his wheel, trundled his car to the road and ran with it in the direction he had come. He pushed it until his breath was coming in gasps. Then he turned into the woods and hid. He would take no chance of being seen by the spy or by any accomplice who might have followed him. Presently Henry heard the motor-car pull out into the road and go speeding back toward Manhattan. A quarter of an hour later Henry returned to the highway, switched on his light, and was soon bowling along on his way to his fellows and his chief, feeling that he had in his keeping the future safety of a nation.

Lewis E. Theiss

CHAPTER XIV

THE RIDDLE SOLVED

In the house above the hawk's nest, four boys and a man sat far into the night, examining a marked dollar and trying to unravel the secret of the scratches. From hand to hand the dollar passed and was examined now this way, now that; but the little group could see no meaning in the apparently aimless marks on the silver coin. Had some of them not seen this dollar marked and its message deciphered and sent vibrating through the air, they would have refused to believe that the coin before them carried a message at all. It looked like any dollar that has accidentally become marked.

"To-morrow," said Captain Hardy, "we will turn the dollar over to the secret service, and doubtless their experts will solve the problem quick enough. But I certainly wish we could unravel this thing ourselves. Wouldn't it be an achievement for the wireless patrol!"

"It's going to be," declared Roy positively. "We're going to solve it. We've just got to. We'll show those secret service men that boys are some good after all."

But the word was easier than the deed. Puzzle their brains as they might, search the dollar as they would, they still found no key to the language it spoke.

"Tell me again what the message was," demanded Henry for the twentieth time, and Lew once more passed to Henry the slip of paper on which he had written the message, both in cipher and deciphered, the message he had picked from the air. It read as follows: TRPSLOWAOSEDONBADATSTITY.

T R P S L O
W A O S E D
O N R A D A
T S T I T Y

Long Henry studied the piece of paper, softly reading the message to himself. "Two transports sailed to-day. How did that automobile driver get that message from this dollar?" he asked himself, and again he picked up the coin and turned it in his hand. "If only we had that disc," he sighed, "or a duplicate."

At the word "duplicate," Roy pricked up his ears. "Maybe we can make one," he said.

"Likely!" scoffed Lew.

"You never know till you try," rejoined Roy. Then he turned to Willie and demanded, "What was the disc like that you saw?"

"If I knew, I'd make one," said Willie.

"Well," said Roy in a tone of disgust, "you know whether it was a foot across or not, and whether it was round or square."

"It was round, of course," said Willie, "and the same size as the dollar. I told you that before."

"We can make a disc the size of a dollar, anyway, even if it doesn't get us anywhere," said Roy, putting the coin on a sheet of paper and outlining it with a pencil. Then with scissors he cut the disc out.

"You saw that disc, or one like it, Henry," continued Roy. "What did it look like to you?"

"Just like a spider-web, as Willie says," replied Henry.

"All right, we'll make a spider-web," said Roy.

He seized his pencil, made a dot in the centre of the disc, and from the dot drew straight lines that radiated in different directions. Then he drew a number of concentric circles about his dot.

"I don't see how that helps any," he said, examining his drawing. "Yet that's the kind of thing they used to mark that dollar."

From hand to hand the paper passed, and each boy compared it with the dollar. But none was any the wiser when he had finished. Their leader, meantime, sat with his head in his hands, studiously turning the matter over and over in his mind. For a long time he could make nothing of it.

After a while he looked up. "Let me see that paper," he said.

Roy handed him the little disc. Captain Hardy laid the disc beside the dollar on the table, and painstakingly examined again the marks on the coin. After a time he took a sheet of paper and across it in a row wrote down the letters of the alphabet. Then he picked up the message and made check marks below the letters in his alphabet as he found those letters in the message. When he had gone through the message, his paper looked like this:

```
ABCDEFGHIJKLMNOPQRSTUVWXYZ
/   / /   /   /  / / /  / / /     / /  /
/     /       /           / / /
/         /               / /
                           /
```

He picked it up and studied it. "Four T's," he said, "three S's, three A's, and three O's. That ought to give us a clue."

Again he turned to the dollar and began to study it, turning it slowly round, counting the scratches this way and that, making geometric figures of them. Four heads peered over his shoulder as he worked silently with his pencil.

"I can make nothing of it," he said after a time.

Again he sat in deep thought, his fellows meanwhile once more examining dollar and disc and the figures their leader had made on the paper.

"Four T's," repeated Captain Hardy after an interval. "Surely that ought to give us a clue."

Once more he studied the penciled disc. Then he turned to the dollar and again examined its markings. He suddenly exclaimed, "Here are four scratches in a straight row." His eyes began to shine. Slowly he turned the coin. "And here are three in another row, like this," and he indicated the positions of the scratches on the paper disc. "You notice that each row runs from the centre of the coin toward the edge. Let's see if there are any more rows."

Lewis E. Theiss

Very slowly he turned the dollar. "And there are three in a row," he said, indicating the scratches with his pencil, "and here are three more. You notice that the rows all radiate from the centre, like spokes in a wheel. I believe we are getting somewhere, boys."

"'Like spokes in a wheel,'" repeated Roy to himself. "Rows of letters like spokes in a wheel. Four scratches in one row or spoke—these must be the four T's. Three scratches in these other rows must be O's and A's and S's. I've got it! I've got it!" he suddenly shouted. "There must be as many spokes as there are letters in the alphabet."

"I believe you are right, Roy," said Captain Hardy, looking up with a gleam in his eyes. "That's exactly what I am beginning to think. We'll soon see if you are right. Make me another disc."

With a pocket rule he measured the diameter of the dollar. "Practically an inch and a half," he announced, putting down the figures 1.5 on paper. He multiplied those figures by 3.1416.

"That," said he, pointing to the resulting figures, 4.71+, "represents the circumference of a dollar. Now we'll divide the circumference by 26, the number of letters in the alphabet."

He performed the division. "Eighteen one-hundredths of an inch," he announced. "That's practically a scant fifth of an inch. We'll call it so, anyhow," he continued as he marked off the space on a sheet of paper with his rule. "Each sector," he said, "gets exactly that amount of space on the circumference."

He pulled open the drawer of the desk and began to

rummage through a tray full of pens, pencils, and other drawing materials. "I wonder if there is such a thing as a pair of dividers here," he remarked. And a moment later he exclaimed "Good!" and drew forth the compasses he was looking for.

He set his dividers according to the space he had marked off with his rule, then proceeded to divide the circumference of the new paper disc. When he had gone completely round the disc, he seized pencil and ruler and began to draw lines from centre to circumference—the spokes of his wheel—each spoke running from the dot in the centre to one of the points indicated by the dividers. When he had finished, the disc was divided into twenty-six equal sectors, like tiny pieces of a pie.

"We shall soon know whether you are right or not in your guess, Roy," said Captain Hardy.

He laid the dollar beside the disc and began to copy on the disc the marks on the dollar. "We'll put four marks in this sector," he said, making four dots with his pencil. "They are like those four scratches here," and he pointed to the four marks in a row on the dollar. "They must be four T's. At any rate we'll call this the T sector. On the dollar you notice this row of three scratches—the next sector to the left of the T sector. You remember we had three O's, three A's, and three S's. These three scratches must, therefore, be O's, A's, or S's. Since they are next to the T's, they are doubtless S's. I'll mark the sector so anyway. That gives us the T sector and the S sector. If we are on the right track, then the sector to the left of the S space is the R sector, and so on. I'll mark the disc that way, anyhow."

Slowly he turned the disc around, putting a letter at the bottom of each sector. When he had finished, he had completed the alphabet. About him clustered his four comrades, too deeply interested to speak. They hardly even breathed.

"Take this paper, Roy," said Captain Hardy, "and tell me how many times each letter in the message appears."

Roy took the paper on which Captain Hardy had made his numerical enumeration. "Three A's," he said.

Captain Hardy made three marks in the A sector.

"No B's, no C's, and two D's."

The D's were scored. So they went through the alphabet. When they were done, the markings on the disc were practically a duplicate of those on the dollar, for Captain Hardy studied the dollar each time before marking the paper disc.

"That's it," cried Willie. "That's it exactly."

"It's right so far as it goes, Willie," said their leader, "but we haven't all of it yet. Suppose I hand you a disc with four T's, three S's, two Z's, three L's, and so on. Could you make a message out of it?"

Willie studied the disc on the desk. "No," he said, "I couldn't. I shouldn't know how to arrange the letters to make words out of them."

"Neither would anybody else," continued Captain Hardy. "Those spies have some way of knowing how to tell the order in which to read these letters."

For some time he sat studying the scratches on the dollar.

The four boys were quiet as mice, each trying to solve the problem that stood between them and complete mastery of the cipher.

"You said that the metal disc resembled a spider's web," began Captain Hardy, talking more to himself than to the boys. "We know what the straight lines—the spokes—are for. The concentric circles must be to indicate the order of the letters. Let me see." Again he studied the dollar closely. "Some of these marks are near the centre of the disc, some half-way between centre and circumference, and some close to the outer edge. I believe the secret lies there."

"Listen!" cried Willie of a sudden. "When a spider spins a web, she begins at the centre and works outward. Maybe these spies write their messages in the same way."

"Willie," cried Captain Hardy, "you've hit it exactly. You're as good a reasoner as you are an observer. Now we'll begin at the centre and spin this message outward. What's the first letter?"

"T," said four voices together.

The captain took his dividers and found the scratch nearest the centre of the disc. In the same sector with this scratch were three other scratches in a line.

"It's a T," he announced, "just as it should be."

With his dividers he found the letter next nearest to the centre. It stood alone. "That's a W," he announced.

Rapidly he located the scratch the third nearest to the centre. "And that's an O," he said, looking up with flashing eyes. "We need go no farther. We have the entire secret. We have deciphered their cipher."

A cry of exultation arose.

"To-morrow," continued Captain Hardy, "we will get a piece of transparent celluloid and make a disc like their own. We can ink in the circles and the radius lines and our disc will be almost a duplicate of theirs, except that our disc will be solid while their discs have open spaces between the circles. But that is only a detail. We can read their cipher as well as if we had one of their own discs."

"Wait," cried Willie, as his comrades started to cheer again. "What is the scratch on the milled edge of the dollar for?"

"That," replied Captain Hardy, "is to indicate how the disc is to be placed on the dollar. That scratch is exactly between the Z and the A sectors. It shows where the alphabet begins. Now we have their entire secret."

CHAPTER XV

ANOTHER MYSTERY UNRAVELED

A piece of transparent celluloid, furnished by their host from a broken side curtain of his automobile, supplied Captain Hardy with the material needed for making the disc that was to be the key to future communications of the enemy. Carefully he cut the celluloid the size of a dollar, then marked the exact centre of it. Next he clamped the disc on the captured coin. Between the rows of letters he scratched in the straight radius lines—the spokes of a wheel. Then Captain Hardy put the end of one arm of his dividers in the dot at the centre of his disc, and swept the other arm around, scratching a circle just outside the first letter in the message —the innermost T. Examination showed that this circle fell just inside of the second letter in the message—the W. Adjusting his calipers, the draughtsman made a second circle, just outside of this second letter. A third circle fell between the first O and the second T of the message. So Captain Hardy continued, each succeeding circle falling just outside of the succeeding letter in the message. When he had finished, his disc contained twenty-three concentric circles, between which could plainly be seen the bright dots or scratches in the dingy dollar.

"Whew!" said Captain Hardy, as he laid down his dividers.

Lewis E. Theiss

"That's pretty fine work—twenty-three circles within a space of an inch and a half. I'll wager a watchmaker made their pattern for them. The solid parts of their metal discs can't be much larger than these lines I have scratched on the celluloid. You were right when you named it, Willie. The parts of it must be just about as thick as a spider-web."

The boys passed the dollar and its superimposed disc from hand to hand, examining them with eager interest.

"Suppose they wanted to send a message with more than twenty-four letters in it," said Roy. "How could they do it? I'm sure some of the messages we intercepted had more than twenty-four letters in them."

Captain Hardy picked up the disc-covered dollar and studied it intently. "I suppose," he said after a time, "that they would put more than one dot in the same circle, and the dots would be read in the same way they are now. The one to be read first would be nearest the centre of the coin, and so on. Or they could write on several coins, each coin being numbered in some way, and corresponding to a paragraph in a composition."

Again he studied the dollar closely. "Clever!" he said admiringly. "Mighty clever! Who would ever dream that those tiny scratches meant anything? Many a time I've seen a dollar scratched and nicked a deal worse than this one is, though they've evidently chosen a battered one so that their own marks will be less noticeable. Why, that coin might have passed through our hands a hundred times, and if we had not actually seen it marked we should never dream it said anything other than 'In God We Trust.' We've had a great stroke of luck, boys."

He paused and meditated. "I wonder if it is luck," he went

on. "May not the motto on that dollar explain our good fortune? Perhaps it is Providence rather than blind luck that has guided us. At any rate let us hope so. Now I'm going to report to the Chief. Won't he get a surprise?"

And Captain Hardy left his subordinates, chuckling at the prospect of the Chief's astonishment.

But it was Captain Hardy who had the surprise. Instead of the stern, silent, brusque man he had become accustomed to, Captain Hardy found the Chief smiling and talkative. As his eye fell on Captain Hardy, the Chief rubbed his hands with apparent satisfaction. Evidently something had happened that had put him in an extremely good humor.

"Ah! Captain Hardy," he said, "we beat you to it this time. I already know what you have come to tell me. But I am glad to see you just the same. One of our operators," continued the Chief, "happened to be shifting his tuning-coil when our friends, the enemy, were sending their message yesterday afternoon, so that I have all the latest spy news."

He paused and smiled at his astonished visitor. "You see," he added, a real Irish twinkle coming into his eyes, "the secret service is not so slow after all."

"Congratulations!" cried Captain Hardy, in the same spirit of fun. "The secret service is improving. But I have some news that may make my trip not altogether without interest to you."

The Chief interrupted him. "We know who the man is that has been telephoning to your Staten Island grocer about sugar," he said. "When he called up yesterday afternoon, the telegraph operator flashed the tip to my man, who happened to be on duty within a few doors of the place the man was

Lewis E. Theiss

talking from. Of course my man spotted him and trailed him. The fellow proves to be a clerk on one of the piers where transports are loading. His position gives him no opportunity to get aboard the ships, so he does not know what goes into the transports. But he does know how many boats are loading and about when they will sail. Evidently he is afraid to telephone directly to any of the better known German agents we are watching, and as far as that goes he may not even know who they are. I suppose this plan of communicating with Staten Island is to give the spy there a chance to observe the transports as they sail from the harbor, and see if he can learn anything about their cargoes. We have put this steamship clerk under observation and from now on he will be watched night and day. We're closing in on them fast."

"Congratulations!" cried Captain Hardy again, this time in sober earnest. "You are doing excellent work. Now when you hear what we—"

Again the Chief interrupted him. "Oh! I haven't told you all *my* news yet, not by a long shot," he said. And again the head of the secret service rubbed his hands together. "We know who the driver of the wireless motor-car is. I don't mean we know the name he's using. Anybody could get that out of a directory. It's Sanders. But we know who he really is. And that's why we feel so good to-day. He's a man we've been looking for for months. He is one of the German agents implicated in the papers we seized in Wolf von Igel's office. The secret service has been more than anxious to discover his whereabouts. Now we have him, for he's under observation and cannot escape us.

"He came to this country about a year before the war started," continued the Chief, a gleam of satisfaction shining in his eyes, "and bought out an insurance agent who made a specialty of insuring suburban properties. From the beginning, he made a practice of visiting the properties that he insured. This took him about a good deal and gave him an excuse for being so much in a motor-car. Ah! What an ideal situation for a spy! Clever, aren't they?"

But the Chief gave his visitor no chance to reply to his query. Smiling again, he went on, "But even this is not all. Of course you understand, Captain, that your boys are not the only amateurs helping us out in this pinch. Ever since we became convinced that the Germans have a line of secret wireless stations by which they are relaying news to their agents in Mexico—for we're morally certain that is where these messages go—we've had trusted amateurs helping us just as you have helped us—by listening in. Some of them have been at it for weeks. When we could get no trace of secret messages along the direct route to Mexico, where they would naturally have their stations, we began to suspect that the Germans were using a round-about route in the hope of deceiving us completely."

"And you've located some of them?"

"Exactly. Your boys will tell you that yesterday was one of those days when radio communication is at its best—when an operator picks up sounds that at other times he could not possibly hear. The result was that we picked up yesterday's secret message at half a dozen different points. Where do you think the first one was?"

"Give it up."

"Buffalo—north instead of south. Clever, eh? Then we got it near Detroit, and Milwaukee, and Omaha, and Santa Fe. Finally one of our listeners picked it up at Socorro, a place about one hundred and seventy miles north of El Paso. Now we know the line of their stations. We'll set a regiment of amateurs to listening in along that line and we'll locate every station in it in no time. Then we'll grab all their agents at the same time in one big raid and wipe out this spy system for good."

"That is great news," said Captain Hardy, his eyes sparkling with interest. "Great! You certainly have cause to feel good."

"For a little while," replied the Chief, "I thought I had even more good news. But it proved to be a false alarm."

"What was it?" inquired Captain Hardy as the Chief stopped speaking.

"Oh! Simply this. Some time ago one of our listeners caught an earlier message near Socorro, which gave us a hint as to where the messages were crossing the border. We at once sent a number of expert army wireless men into that part of the border region to listen in. One message was picked up at a point fifty miles north of the boundary, but it was very faint. Along the line itself the radio men have never detected a sound. Yet your boys are intercepting the messages here, so we know that they are being sent regularly. That made us think that perhaps the messages were being telephoned the last lap of the journey and carried over the line by a person."

"I have no doubt that your theory is correct," said Captain Hardy.

"Well, last night we thought for a time that we had the man who was carrying the messages. When my operator here picked up the message yesterday afternoon, I instantly sent a message to my subordinate in charge of the work in the El Paso district, telling him of the sending of the message and urging extra vigilance. Yet not one of the radio men heard a sound. But in the middle of the night my men grabbed a

Mexican who had slipped past the armed guards and was starting to wade across the Rio Grande to Mexico."

"Excellent!" cried Captain Hardy.

"Good enough as far as it went," said the Chief, with a wry face, "but it didn't go far enough. The fellow was only a smuggler."

"Are you certain, Chief?"

"Sure as preaching, worse luck."

"Was the man searched thoroughly?"

"Now, Captain, what do you think the secret service is, anyway? Was he searched! It would make your eyes pop out if you'd see the way we go through a man. We strip him and give him a lemon bath to bring out any secret message that might be written on his skin, and we take his clothes apart scientifically, I tell you. No, this fellow had nothing incriminating on him. After a grueling examination, he admitted that he had crossed the line to smuggle in some tobacco. However, it's only a question of time until we *do* put our finger on the missing link. Then for a great raid!"

"How I shall welcome that day," said Captain Hardy. "This spy business is never absent from my thoughts, with its menace to our boys on the ocean."

"I think that you will soon be free to go back to the army," said the Chief. "Your work is about done. This thing is coming to a head fast now. But of course I shall need your boys to listen in for a time, so that we can know what the Germans are sending. But there will probably be no more real work for you. We certainly are grateful for the help you gave us, though. We have been terribly crowded these last few weeks."

In his pride at the work his boys had done, Captain Hardy momentarily forgot the errand that had brought him to the Chief's office. He stood before the head of the secret service, smiling happily. Again he began to think of that long chain of secret wireless stations, so sinister and so menacing, with voice crying treachery to voice through the air, carrying word that at any time might cause the murder of thousands of our brave soldiers. Mentally he journeyed along the line of those stations—from New York to Buffalo, to Detroit, to Milwaukee, to Omaha, to Santa Fe, to Socorro, to Mexico. With quick imagination he pictured the scores of little secret stations needed to carry those treacherous messages across so vast a span of earth. Some he saw skilfully hidden in forests, as the wireless had been concealed at the Elk City reservoir. Some he pictured in abandoned farmhouses. Others he saw in barns, in the stacks of ruined factories. And some he imagined as flinging their voices abroad amid the burning plains of the arid border-lands. But he could not picture to himself the invisible messenger that took the word across the boundary. He could not fathom the mystery, he could not picture to himself the missing link in the chain. As was always the case with him, his mind began at once to grapple with its problem—in this instance the riddle of the missing link. He actually forgot where he was.

"I wonder," he said, though he was really talking to himself, "what was done with that smuggler."

"We clapped him into jail to await trial for smuggling," said the Chief.

Captain Hardy came to himself with a start, and smiled. "You say they got nothing incriminating on him," he remarked. "Did your men find anything at all?"

"Only the money he had gotten for his tobacco."

Mechanically Captain Hardy had thrust his hand into his pocket. As the Chief answered the question, Captain Hardy's fingers came in contact with a silver dollar and a disc of celluloid. Of a sudden an eager light flashed into his eyes. "What kind of money did that Mexican have?" he demanded.

"Some silver," said the Chief indifferently.

"Of what denominations?"

"Dollars. He had three of them."

"What was done with that money?" asked the captain with an earnestness that was almost tragic.

"Oh! The greaser made such a disturbance that the jailer let him keep it. He's got it with him in the jail."

A great sigh burst from Captain Hardy's lips. "Telegraph your men instantly," he cried, "to get those dollars. That Mexican is no smuggler. He's a spy. He's the man who carries the messages across the border. The messages are on the dollars. And here's the key to the cipher!"

And he drew from his pocket and laid before the Chief a battered silver dollar and a curiously marked celluloid disc.

Lewis E. Theiss

CHAPTER XVI

AN UNEXPECTED MESSAGE

"Was he surprised?" cried the four boys of the wireless patrol, as their captain entered the living-room after his trip to the secret service offices.

Captain Hardy chuckled. "I think he was," he said. "But for a time it was I who was surprised. The Chief knew from his own men all about yesterday's message. One of them picked it up. What's more, he has a lot of amateurs in different parts of the country listening in, just as you are doing, and they picked up yesterday's message at enough different points to indicate the line of the secret stations we are after. The messages are crossing the border somewhere near El Paso. But the Germans are getting them across in some way other than by wireless. They know we'd spot their outfit quick. The Chief thinks some one telephones the messages the last lap and that a messenger carries them into Mexico."

"And what about the dollar and the disc?" asked Roy. "What did the Chief think of them?"

"Well, he was surprised. And what's more, we got hold of that dollar at exactly the right moment. The secret service men arrested a Mexican who was wading the Rio Grande at

El Paso last night. They searched him and found nothing on him that seemed incriminating. They questioned him and the fellow finally said he had smuggled some tobacco into this country, so they put him in jail as a smuggler. The fellow had some money he had gotten for his tobacco—and it was three silver dollars! The secret service men down there knew nothing of what we have found out here, so they gave the fellow back his money. But I am morally certain that their man is the spy who carries the messages across the border."

"Of course," cried Willie. "What else could he be—sneaking across the boundary with three silver dollars."

Everybody laughed.

"It doesn't follow that he's a spy, just because he has three silver dollars. He may be a smuggler, all right enough. But I believe the smuggling is just a blind. If he were a genuine smuggler, he'd bring more than three dollars' worth of stuff across."

"What have they done with his dollars now?" asked Roy eagerly.

"I don't know, Roy. The Chief got into instant touch with his men at El Paso as soon as I showed him the dollar Henry got. But I left before I knew what the outcome was. However, I have no doubt they will find that the dollars are what we suspect them to be."

"Gee!" said Willie. "To think that the wireless patrol found out about those dollars!"

"I guess the secret service knows by this time that boys are worth something," smiled Roy. "Before we get through, they may think so even more."

"You're certainly not increasing in modesty," laughed their leader.

"Well, I don't care," said Roy hotly. "It makes me tired. Everybody says, 'Oh! They're only boys.' Of course we're only boys, but look at what we've done. Why, the wireless patrol has got the best set of fellows—"

But Roy's protest was smothered in a burst of laughter from his fellows.

"Well, I'm glad you feel so good over what we've been fortunate enough to accomplish," said Captain Hardy, "for I fear there will be no more excitement for you. The Chief says his men now have the spy business well in hand, and that all he wants of us from now on is merely to stay here and catch their messages until he is ready to make his raid."

"Just what I was saying," burst out Roy indignantly. "They won't let us in on their raid because 'we're only boys.' But who was it caught the dynamiters, if it wasn't 'just boys'? The men couldn't do it. They tried twice and failed. Gee! It makes me tired."

"Never mind, Roy," said Captain Hardy smiling. "Even if we don't have any further taste of excitement, we can always remember that we had a big part in catching these spies—for they're going to be caught, sure. And you mustn't forget that if we stay here and do well the part assigned to us, we are helping just as much as the men who actually round up the spies. You know Milton says 'They also serve who only stand and wait.' If there aren't any reserves to stand and wait behind the lines, the men on the firing-line do not dare to push ahead. And besides, Roy, it is seldom that four boys play so important a part in great deeds as you four boys already have played."

"Four boys and a man," corrected Henry. "Without you we could never have gotten anywhere," and Henry looked affectionately at his captain.

"Oh! Yes, I had a part in it," agreed the captain, "but it was only a part."

"But you read the ciphers," protested Henry. "If you hadn't done that, we could not have made any headway at all."

"And who caught the messages for me to decipher? The reason we have gotten along so well is because we work together so perfectly. I want to thank you boys for being so faithful. I've given you many hard tasks to do."

"After our experiences at Camp Brady," said Lew, "we couldn't do anything else than be faithful. We know by experience what happens when we don't do our duty."

"Then you are going to listen in during the remainder of the spy hunt," said Captain Hardy, with an affectionate smile, "just as faithfully as though your work weren't already done and the spice gone out of it. I know it will be dull and uninteresting, boys, but you've made such a fine record that I don't want you to fall down now. So be very careful—if only for my sake."

"They've never talked once," said Henry ruefully, "excepting after the transports sail. I don't suppose they ever will except when the ships go out. We'll have to listen to nothing for twenty-four hours a day. But we're going to do it just the same."

He rose and walked toward the wireless room. "It's back to the mines for me," he added. And he disappeared through the doorway of the wireless room.

But hardly had he sat down and clamped the receiver to his ears before he cried out. His fellows came flocking into the room. Henry was swiftly writing a string of letters on a sheet of paper.

"Something of moment must be afoot," said Captain Hardy, in a low voice, "for them to be talking at this time. It must be important, indeed."

"It's a long message," whispered Willie, as Henry continued to fashion letter after letter.

"Something tells me it is important," repeated Captain Hardy. "What can it be? You don't suppose the secret service men have alarmed them, do you?"

Henry finished his writing and laid down his pencil. His chief picked up the sheet of paper and scanned the long line of letters Henry had made, like this:

EEANNRDBOEUNRYWSEUTTERONSNNFEEIAYW
MNVTTASANXJULEIGOKWSNVATYIZLETK

"Sixty-five," he said aloud, after counting the letters carefully.

A frown came over his face as he stood looking at the paper in his hand. "Sixty-five," he repeated. "All their other cipher messages have made four even lines. You can't divide sixty-five evenly by four. Boys, I believe—but we'll make sure first."

He sank into a chair, laid the paper on the desk, and arranged the letters according to the old plan, thus:

EEANNRDBOEUNRYW

SEUTTERONSNNFEE
IAYWMNVTTASANXJ
ULEIGOKWSNVATYI

"I don't know what to do with the five letters left over," he said, as he laid down his pencil. Then as he ran his eye down column after column and across each line, he continued, "But I guess it makes no difference. It is just as I thought. I feel more certain than ever that something of great importance is afoot. They've switched to another cipher."

CHAPTER XVII

A CHANGE IN CIPHERS

For some moments there was a complete silence in the room. The members of the wireless patrol looked at one another in astonishment, questioning with their eyes the meaning of this new turn of events. Captain Hardy sat staring at the message before him, his brow wrinkled, his eyelids drawn close together, trying to find some new clue to the puzzle before him. And until he spoke, the lads of the little patrol forbore to utter a sound. So for some time the room remained as silent as a tunnel.

At last the captain glanced up from his paper and noted the intent looks bent upon him, and the deep silence. He shook off his abstraction.

"It looks as though we were up against it," he said. "Every minute I feel more certain that something serious has happened. Why should they be sending radio messages at this hour, when they have never sent them before excepting after the transports sailed? And why should they now use a new cipher? Their plan evidently was to use radio communication as little as possible, lest they be detected. So they sent nothing by wireless but the most important news—the news of ship movements, which had to be got to Germany at once.

All other messages they conveyed in some slower but safer way. We know they used the telephone, and sent messages by a boy, and wrote on dollars, and carried messages by motor-car, and probably sent code letters through the mails. For all ordinary correspondence they used these slower, safer methods. Only when they absolutely had to, did they employ the wireless. So we must assume that they had to now."

He paused and glanced from face to face. "But why the change of cipher?" he continued. "It must be because they fear that the old cipher will be understood."

Again the captain fell silent. "What can have happened?" he inquired soberly, "that makes the use of wireless so imperative? What can it be? Only something new and unforeseen. And what could there be new and unforeseen except the detection of their plot? More and more I am convinced that these plotters have been alarmed."

He fell into a brown study for a moment. "This message can mean nothing else," he said after a little. "It is imperative that we learn what it is at the earliest possible moment. Make four copies of the message you took, Henry."

Captain Hardy's first lieutenant took the paper from his leader's hand and on four sheets of paper copied the string of letters he had picked from the air.

"Now, boys," said the leader of the patrol, when the copies were complete, "put your thinking caps on. Each of you take one of these copies and see what you can make of it. You know how we deciphered the other cipher."

In another moment four boys were wrinkling their foreheads as they bent over the cryptic strings of letters. And over the room came a hush deep as midnight's.

For a few moments nobody broke the silence. Each boy was busy with his own thoughts.

Henry was scowling at his paper. Willie was studying the letters before him, as in earlier days he had studied the landscapes about Camp Brady and the Elk City reservoir. Lew already had a hopeless look on his face. At threading the forest he was second to none in skill; but at untangling mental puzzles, he had small ability. The nimble-witted Roy was already setting about his task with that keenness so characteristic of him.

"Sixty-five letters," he said to himself. "If this cipher is anything like the other, those letters must be arranged in columns of equal size."

For a second he sat scanning the letters. Then he muttered, "What will divide sixty-five evenly?" And a moment later, he answered his own query by adding, "Five, and thirteen."

He paused and again ran his eye along the row of letters. "If this cipher works like the other there must be five rows of thirteen letters each, or thirteen rows of five each. I'll try the five rows first. That's more like the other cipher."

Swiftly he set down the five rows of letters, thus:

```
E E A N N R D B O E U N R
Y W S E U T T E R O N S N
N F E E I A Y W M N V T T
A S A N X J U L E I G O K
W S N V A T Y I Z L E T K
```

Eagerly he ran his eye down the columns of letters, as he had become accustomed to doing with the old cipher, but the letters were unintelligible. Next he read the letters across the rows, but with no better result. The eager look faded from his eyes.

"I'll have to try the other," he said, and began to make his letters into rows of five each, thus:

```
E E A N N
R D B O E
U N R Y W
S E U T T
E R O N S
N N F E E
I A Y W M
N V T T A
S A N X J
 U L E I G
O K W S N
V A T Y I
Z L E T K
```

With renewed eagerness he ran his eye down the first column. "E-R-U-S-E-N-I-N—" he began, then stopped short in disgust. "Nothing doing that way," he muttered.

Then he read the letters across the rows: "E-E-A-N-N—"

"They've got me stopped," he said. And he threw down his pencil and sat staring at the paper before him, twisting the letters into every shape he could think of, but to no avail.

Meantime each of the other members of the patrol was going through much the same process. Lew gave up first, acknowledging himself beaten. Henry sat scowling and working away industriously. Dr. Hardy tried first one combination of letters, then another, but in vain. Willie had laid out the letters in exactly the same way Roy had. But Willie worked differently from any boy in the group. The rest had been feverishly setting down letters as new combinations presented themselves to their minds, whether the combinations seemed logical or not. Willie first arranged his letters in the long rows and sat for many minutes looking intently at them.

At Camp Brady it was Willie who had learned, better than any other member of the patrol, the lesson of observation. When the patrol was practising scouting, which is only another name for close observing, Willie had sat for hours studying the landscapes, even when his fellows teased him. Thus he had learned to see everything within sight and make note of it. And when a guide was needed later, to conduct a party through the midnight woods in quest of the dynamiters' lair, Willie was the scout who was able to do it. He had observed perfectly and so carefully noted what he saw that even in the darkness he could find his way.

So now he examined his long rows of letters until he knew everything about them; and he was certain they told no story. When he was certain, he rearranged the letters, as Roy had done, in rows of five each. Then he laid down his pencil and began another careful search. He read the topmost line from left to right, and from right to left. It made no sense. He took the second and found no meaning in it. Another boy might have skipped the others, but not Willie. Each of the thirteen rows he studied forward and backward.

Then he ran his eye down the first column, just as Roy had done. It spelled nothing. But when he began at the bottom and came upward, an eager light leaped into his eyes. He could make nothing of the lowest five letters; but the eight above certainly spelled two words: "nine sure." If the message was in English, Willie knew he had found something definite to work on. He could make nothing of the second column, either upward or downward. But the third column gave him distinctly the words "twenty four." The next column yielded more words: "Six twenty."

By this time Willie's eyes were flashing. He turned to the bottom of the last column and began to read upward. A single glance confirmed his suspicion.

"Captain Hardy," he cried, jumping over to his chief, and laying his paper on the captain's desk, "begin at the bottom of the last column and read upward. I believe this cipher is exactly the opposite of the other."

Willie's fellows dropped their pencils and gathered eagerly about their leader as he slowly read the letters, beginning at the bottom of the last column and reading upward and backward in the exact opposite of the way the former messages had been deciphered.

"K," he read, "I-N-G-J-A-M-E-S-T-W-E-N-T-Y-S-I-X-T-W-E-N-T-Y-O-N-E-T-W-E-N-T-Y-F-O-U-R-B-A-L-A-K-L-A-V-A-N-R-E-N-D-E-Z-V-O-U-S-N-I-N-E-S-U-R-E."

"Hurrah for Willie!" cried Roy, who had been putting down the letters as Captain Hardy read them off. "He's solved the problem. Who says boys aren't any good? I'll bet you—"

But Roy was interrupted by his mates. "Read it to us," they demanded.

"It's a funny message," said Roy, and slowly he read the following: "King James twenty six twenty one twenty four—" Then he stopped. "I can't read the next words," he said.

Captain Hardy took the paper from Roy and read the entire message. "King James twenty six twenty one twenty four Balaklavan rendezvous nine sure."

"What a queer message," said Henry. "What does it mean?"

"It means," said Captain Hardy, "that the Germans have done their very best to deceive us. They not only changed their cipher, but they sent their message in code. We have read their cipher, but we know no more than we did before. We can never work out their code. All we can do is to guess at the meaning. Our difficulties, instead of being ended, are just beginning. I am more and more convinced that this message is important."

CHAPTER XVIII

TOO LATE

The look of astonishment that appeared on every face at the reading of the message was soon succeeded by one of bewilderment.

"How are we ever going to find out what it means?" demanded Willie. "We can keep juggling letters around until we get them into the proper combinations to make words out of them. But here we've got the words. And they don't mean anything to us. And I don't see how we're ever going to find out what they do mean. We couldn't juggle words around, too, could we, Captain Hardy?"

"No, Willie. There is no use trying that. The spies know what the words mean, all right enough. And nobody else does, unless he has the key to the code. All we can do is to guess what they mean."

"It will take some tall guessing," laughed Roy. "I don't even know what two of those words mean. Read 'em, Willie—those two long ones."

Everybody laughed. "B-A-L-A-K-L-A-V-A-N R-E-N-D-E-Z-V-O-U-S," spelled Willie. "They've got me stopped, too.

What do they mean, Captain Hardy?"

"Balaklavan evidently is an adjective referring to Balaklava. Does any one of you remember that word? You've had it in history."

"I know," said Henry. "That's where the Light Brigade made its famous charge in the Crimean War."

"Good," said Captain Hardy. "That's exactly right. So that word evidently refers to a famous battle-ground. Can it be that we have stumbled on a diplomatic message instead of one meant for these spies? Could it be that this message has anything to do with the situation in the Balkans, I wonder?" and Captain Hardy began to turn the matter over in his mind.

"You didn't tell us what that other word meant," said Roy.

"Oh!" said the captain, with a smile. "That's a word of French origin that means meeting-place. Balaklavan meeting-place, Balaklavan meeting-place," repeated the captain. "This certainly must be an important message. The Chief ought to know about it at once. But I wouldn't dare telephone it. I'd have to take it to him."

"Maybe *we* could find out what it means," said Roy, "if only you would stay to direct us. Wouldn't it be great if the wireless patrol—"

"Roy," interrupted the patrol leader, "I know how you feel. You are very loyal to the wireless patrol. But this is a case that calls for loyalty to Uncle Sam first. The important thing is to get the message read—not to have it read by any particular persons."

"Let me take the message to the Chief," suggested Lew. "I

am no good at this sort of thing, but I can carry a message as fast as anybody. Then you could stay here and help the others."

"Very well, Lew. Take a copy of the message as we caught it, and a copy of the cipher as we arranged it. The Chief will learn as much from them as he would from half an hour's talk. Now hurry."

In a few minutes Lew was speeding toward Manhattan with the message in his pocket, while the remainder of the wireless patrol were drawn up about Captain Hardy's desk, in earnest consultation.

"If only we had an up-to-date history," sighed Henry. "Then we'd know who the sovereigns are in the Balkans. All I know are Peter, of Servia, and it seems to me that he abdicated or died; and Ferdinand, of Bulgaria; and Constantine, of Greece, who abdicated in favor of his son Alexander; and the king of Roumania—isn't his name Ferdinand, too?"

"Then there is Charles, of Austria," suggested Captain Hardy, "and the Turkish Sultan, and King Victor Emmanuel III, of Italy. But I can't think of any King James. Well, we'll drop the kings at present and go on with the cipher. That brings us to three groups of letters—twenty-six, twenty-one, twenty-four. I know that code makers frequently use arbitrary groups of letters or figures to represent given words or ideas, but I haven't the slightest notion as to whether these figures belong together or are to be read separately. And as to what they mean, we can only guess. Since they seem to be in connection with some ruler and something about a Balkan meeting-place, they might refer to troops. You don't suppose the Germans are massing forces for another drive into Roumania or that part of Russia around the Black Sea, do you?"

Lewis E. Theiss

For a little time there was complete silence, as each member of the party struggled to remember all that he had read about the situation in the near East. But none could throw any light on the matter.

"Well, we will drop the numbers and go on," said Captain Hardy. "That brings us back to the Balaklavan rendezvous. The word rendezvous plainly indicates some kind of a meeting. A number of people are going to get together somewhere. If the place indicated were not so evidently in the Crimea, I should think that the message might mean that these German agents we've been watching are summoned to a meeting somewhere."

Again there was a long pause. "Henry," said Captain Hardy suddenly, "to whom was this message sent, and by whom?"

"It had the same call signals that have always been used. It must have been sent from the motor-car station and it is intended for the same station or stations the other messages were sent to. But we don't know yet where they are."

"What would this motor-car driver, Sanders, be sending out a message about the Balkans for?" demanded Henry. "Is he connected with the German diplomatic corps as well as with the spy activities?"

"That's exactly what I was wondering about," replied Captain Hardy. "I can make nothing of it. The only thing I can under-stand is the last part of the message—'nine sure.' Somebody is to meet somebody somewhere at nine o'clock sure."

"If they meet at the Balaklavan rendez—What's that word? I can't remember, Captain Hardy," said Roy.

"Rendezvous."

"Well, if somebody is to meet at some place at nine o'clock, the place can't be in the Balkans—not if the people who meet are the persons who received this message."

"You're right, Roy. And they couldn't meet in Europe, or even very far away in the United States, for," he continued, glancing at his watch, "it is already long past luncheon time."

"Well," said Henry, "there wouldn't be any sense in telling these spies about a meeting in the Balkans, anyway. So the message must be intended to call them to a meeting themselves."

"It must be so," assented Captain Hardy. "And if it is so, the situation is serious. Why should they want to meet? And why should the need be so urgent that they can't wait to send their message by safer channels, but fling it out into the air for anybody to pick up and read, if he has brains enough to do it? Hello! Here's Lew back again." And turning to the new member of the group, the leader said, "What did the Chief think of your message?"

"He was as puzzled as we were. He said his cipher experts were as busy as they could be with wireless messages of the utmost importance that the Germans had sent from Brazil to Berlin and that government operators had intercepted. But just as soon as he can get a man who knows anything about ciphers and codes, he will put him at this job."

"Then it's all the more important that we should unravel this thing ourselves. If something is to be done at nine o'clock, we haven't a moment to lose."

Hastily they ate their luncheon, then filed back to their living-room, where lay their maps, books, guides, and other equipment.

Lewis E. Theiss

"We had better clear off these tables and desks," said Captain Hardy, "so that we shall have plenty of desk room. Suppose you pile these books on that book-shelf there, Henry. And you, Willie, put those maps on the mantel over the fireplace."

Henry gathered up a huge armful of books and hastily dumped them on the book-shelf indicated. They slid down into a heap, but none fell to the floor. Henry, in his usual careful manner, began to set the books to rights.

"Never mind that now," exclaimed Captain Hardy. "That can wait until we have more time."

Willie, meanwhile, was hastily stacking maps on the mantelpiece. He did not bother to fold them up, but put a weight on them and let the sheets hang down toward the floor. In no time the desks were cleared, and the little group soberly seated before them.

"You've taken away the paper with the message on it," said Captain Hardy to Henry.

Henry started for the book-shelves, but Willie, who sat nearest the shelves, was there almost before Henry was out of his chair. He scanned the heap of books, looking for the missing paper.

"There it is, under that Bible," he muttered.

He lifted off the superimposed books, and shoved the Bible to one side. The books began to slide, but Willie stopped them before they poured down to the floor. The Bible he caught on the very edge of the shelf, its covers open. He thrust the book back, seized the paper, and returned to his seat.

For perhaps an hour the little group worked on. Sometimes each labored in silence, busy with his own thoughts. Again there was eager discussion, as one or the other advanced some theory or idea as to the meaning of the message. Then silence would come again. So the hours rolled by. In one of these pauses, Willie sat with closed eyes, turning the mystery over in his mind. But his brain was tired and other thoughts would creep in. Once he caught himself thinking of Camp Brady. Again he was thinking about the East River, and all the sights he had seen on a trip he had made up that stream into the Sound. Rigidly he brought himself back to his task. But presently his attention wandered again. Now he was thinking about the book-shelf and the volume he had caught as it was slipping to the floor. And then, as though a flash of lightning had suddenly illuminated a dark place in his brain, he saw the words on the open page of the book—words that in his haste he had barely glimpsed, but that now came vividly to his mind:

TO THE MOST HIGH AND MIGHTY PRINCE

JAMES,
By the Grace of God
King of Great Britain, etc.

In another instant Willie was on his feet. "There's one King James that we didn't think of," he said, "the King James of the Bible."

His fellows laughed. "He's dead," said Roy.

But Willie paid no attention to the comment. His look was centred on his captain's face. And his captain's face was worth watching. Over it came that eager look that always marked his countenance when he got new light on a problem.

Lewis E. Theiss

"Willie," he said, "I can't see the connection offhand, but it may well be that there is one. Can anybody think of any connection between King James and Balaklava and these spies?"

Nobody could. "The only thing that King James is remembered for," continued Captain Hardy, "is this very Bible—the King James' version, as we call it, in contradistinction to the Revised version. But I don't quite see how we can connect him with the rest of the message. Read the message over again, Henry."

When Henry had read it, Roy said, "If it said Matthew, or Psalms instead of King James, you would think that it was a text."

Captain Hardy leaped to his feet. "Stupid!" he cried. "Why didn't I see it before? Of course it's a text. Bring me the Bible. King James, 26, 21, 24," muttered Captain Hardy, as Roy placed it before him. "That must indicate the book, chapter, and verse."

He turned to the table of contents and began to count the books of the Bible. "Ezekiel," he announced, when he reached twenty-six. "If our theory is correct, this message refers to Ezekiel 21, 24. We'll soon know whether we're right or not."

His fingers trembled as he turned the pages, so eager was he. He found Ezekiel, turned to the twenty-first chapter, and ran his shaking finger down the columns until it rested on the twenty-fourth verse.

"Listen," he said, and his companions scarcely breathed as he read: "'Therefore thus saith the Lord God, Because ye have made your iniquity to be remembered, in that your transgressions are discovered, so that in all your doings your sins do appear; because, I say, that ye are come to remembrance, ye shall be taken with the hand.'"

For an instant complete silence followed the reading. Then Captain Hardy said, "Willie, you've solved the riddle. And it is just as I feared. The Germans have been alarmed. They know that they are detected. Now everything is plain enough —in a way. They had to warn all the members of the gang and they hadn't time to send messages. So they took a chance on the wireless. But they used a new cipher and resorted to a code. The use of the word 'rendezvous' indicates to my mind that they intend to flee. They're going to meet at the 'Balaklavan rendezvous' at nine. We've got to find where that is and get the secret service men there in time to nab them. And the afternoon's almost gone already."

Captain Hardy pulled out his watch and groaned as he looked at it. "We've got to watch these spies, too," he said. "Above all things we mustn't let them get away from us. If we can't find out where the Balaklavan rendezvous is any other way, we can trail these fellows to it."

Then the leader of the scouts turned to Lew. "Hustle down to the pine tree," he directed, "and watch the hawk's nest. It may already be too late. But if anybody is still there and comes out, trail him no matter where he goes. You can get into touch with me by telephone. Meantime, I'll communicate with the Chief."

Lew hurried away and Captain Hardy left the room to telephone. He came back with a white face.

"The Chief hasn't a man available," he reported. "All his men are watching some plotters who are trying to burn grain elevators and fire shipping. He says it's up to us and the police. So I called Police Headquarters and two detectives will be sent here at once. Pray Heaven they come in time."

Hardly had he finished speaking before Lew burst into the room. "Captain Hardy," he cried, "I was too late. Just as I reached the pine grove, I saw the spy running down the slope. He was a quarter of a mile away. I ran after him. But before I got near the shore he stepped into a motor-boat that was waiting and away he went. There were three other persons in the boat, and I am sure one was the grocer and one his boy. I had no way of following them, so I came straight back."

Just then the door-bell rang. Their hostess announced two men to see Captain Hardy. And the two detectives entered.

"Too late," groaned Captain Hardy. "The birds have flown. And we do not know where they have gone."

CHAPTER XIX

THE ENEMY ESCAPES

Evidently the detectives were little interested in the case. They asked a few perfunctory questions and went away without making any effort to intercept the fleeing motor-boat.

"They remind me of those state police at the Elk City reservoir," said Roy indignantly, "They don't take any interest in anything they don't do themselves. Or maybe they think the matter isn't worth bothering with because we're only boys."

"No, Roy," explained Captain Hardy, "I think it must be because we're working with the secret service. The police and the secret service are as jealous of each other as two cats; and the police don't want to do anything that will bring any credit to the secret service. They might have been able to do something to intercept that motor-boat. But I don't know what we can do. What was the boat like, anyway?"

Lew was able to give a good description of it; but evidently all distinguishing marks had been removed from it. It was a craft of perhaps thirty-five feet, slender, of light draft, and quite certainly built for speed. There was no name at either bow or stern, and the boat was painted a muddy gray that made it almost invisible at a little distance, so well did the color harmonize with the color of the harbor waters. Lew had watched it until it was almost out of sight; and all he knew was that it had started straight out through the Narrows, as though bound for the ocean.

"It looks at first glance," said Captain Hardy, "as though they were going to sea; but they couldn't go far in that craft. Perhaps there is some larger vessel there that they hope to reach."

He turned the idea over in his mind for a time. "I think it more likely that they are heading for some point on land," he said. "They are so clever at deception that that is most likely to be the case; and if it is, they may not even be going in the direction they are headed for. It will soon be dark. Then they could double back unseen. It's my idea that Newark ought to be a good refuge for them. It's a pretty big place, and it's full of German sympathizers—and they can reach it the way they're going. All they need to do is to keep right on around this island. That will take them to Newark Bay. I wonder if that isn't what they're up to, anyway?"

Willie went over to the mantel and brought a large map that showed all the waters of the region. He spread it out on the table and the group gathered around it, shoulders together, heads bent low.

"They might be making for Raritan Bay or Jamaica Bay," suggested Henry.

"Yes," replied Captain Hardy, "but I don't think it likely. Quite evidently they fear pursuit, and they will know that they are safest where boats are most numerous. And I should think that would be in Newark Bay, although I don't really know."

"They could coast along the shores of New Jersey," said Henry, "or of Long Island. What would they be most likely to do?"

"Ah!" replied Captain Hardy. "That's the very question. You know what Sherlock Holmes used to say: 'Eliminate the impossible, and whatever remains, no matter how improbable, is the truth.' I think that we can eliminate the possibility of their going to sea. That is practically impossible—unless—unless—there's a ship out there waiting for them. If this were England instead of America, I'd say that's exactly what was afoot: that there was a German boat somewhere offshore waiting for them. But the possibility of there being such a ship here is so remote that we can dismiss it."

"If they aren't going offshore, where are they going?" demanded Lew.

Everybody laughed. "That's what we've got to find out," replied Captain Hardy.

"I don't see how," said Lew hopelessly.

"No more do I," rejoined their leader, "but we'll have to start with what clues we have and try to follow them. All we know is that this motor-boat is outward bound through the Narrows and presumably is going to be at the Balaklavan rendezvous at nine o'clock."

"I wish we had a Light Brigade to send after them," sighed Henry, and as the others laughed, he began to quote what he remembered of Tennyson's lines that have made the name of Balaklava immortal:

Lewis E. Theiss

"Into the jaws of death,
Into the mouth of hell
Rode the six hundred."

Long ago dusk had come. The lights were lighted and the little group of scouts still clustered about their maps, searching vainly for a clue. Their hostess came to call them to dinner.

"I am sorry," said Captain Hardy apologetically, "but we are at work on a very grave matter and cannot possibly stop for dinner. Could you conveniently send us up some coffee and sandwiches?"

So, while they munched their sandwiches and sipped their hot coffee, the members of the wireless patrol continued their search for the missing clue. Occasionally Lew, more restless than his fellows, strolled over to the window and stood gazing out over the harbor, with its entrancing lights.

"There goes the *Patrol*," he called out suddenly, as a boat bearing the distinctive lights of the police department slipped down the Narrows, while he was at the window.

Captain Hardy gave an exclamation of annoyance. "Why didn't I think of that boat?" he said savagely. "We might have been able to follow the motor-boat if we could have gotten the *Patrol* here. For all we know, she may have been near at hand. And she is equipped with wireless, too. Well, it's too late now." Then bitterly he added, "The man who ordered the charge of the Light Brigade wasn't the only one who blundered."

"Is there any place near New York," suddenly demanded Henry, "named Balaklava or Crimea or anything else that suggests Balaklava?"

"Get that atlas from the book-shelves and see, Henry," replied Captain Hardy. "Look through the list of towns, rivers, lakes, etc. And you, Willie, study the map a while. That seems to be your forte. You may find something to suggest Balaklava to you."

Willie laid the map squarely on the table, and while Henry pored over the atlas and the others talked, and thought at intervals, he began a systematic survey of the map. And naturally he began in the region of the Lower Bay, toward which the motor-boat had disappeared.

Minute followed minute. Dusk turned to deep darkness. Captain Hardy opened and shut his watch in desperation. Swiftly the time was drawing near for the meeting of the spies, and the wireless patrol had not only failed at the critical moment, had not only allowed the enemy to escape, but had lost all track of them. It was a bitter thought and Captain Hardy tried to shut it out of his mind and centre attention on the problem in hand. Henry was still poring over names. Willie had finished his methodical examination of the Lower Bay and was working his way northward. He followed the boundaries of the harbor up through the Narrows and along the Jersey shore, then pursued his quest throughout the length and breadth of Newark Bay. But he found nothing suggestive of Balaklava. Back to the Bay he traced his route, then slowly traversed its waters. Past Bayonne, past Bedloe's Island, past Jersey City, and up the Hudson his pencil slowly moved, as he surveyed every name and looked at every turn and angle of the shore. Then he came back to the eastern side of the Narrows and went north along the Brooklyn shore. Past the Erie Basin, past Governor's Island, past the Brooklyn Bridge, past the Navy Yard, past Blackwell's Island, past Ward's Island, past Hell Gate, with its swirling currents, and on into the Sound, he traveled in imagination, examining every point and word on the map, but he saw nothing suggestive.

The minutes crept on. Eight o'clock had already struck. Captain Hardy was in a fever of anxiety. He could no longer sit still, but was pacing the floor. Lew, utterly hopeless of helping, stood at the window, looking out over the myriad lights of the harbor.

"There's the *Patrol*," he said. "She's coming back up the Narrows."

"If we only knew where to go, it wouldn't be too late yet," said Captain Hardy in a tragic voice. "It is awful to think that we have failed." In an agony of mind he began to pace the floor.

Henry had finished his perusal of the atlas and was thinking desperately over the problem. "I'd gladly go where the Light Brigade went," he muttered, "if only it would take us to those spies." And again he began to quote:

"Into the jaws of death,
Into the mouth of hell
Rode the six hundred."

Hardly had he finished, when Willie gave a loud cry. "Hell Gate!" he almost shrieked. "That's where they are going to meet."

Captain Hardy stopped abruptly in his walk. The flush of hope crept into his cheek. "It's far-fetched," he said, "but it may be. It's the only chance we've got. Can we make it in time? Where's the *Patrol*, Lew?"

"Right there, sir; almost out of the Narrows."

"Quick, Henry. The wireless."

Henry rushed to the wireless room. Captain Hardy strode after him. The others followed. With eager, skilful fingers, Henry adjusted his instrument and began to flash out the call for the police-boat.

Almost at once he got an answer. As Henry wrote down the letters, Captain Hardy leaned over his shoulder, his eyes fastened on Henry's pencil.

"Tell them the secret service needs them at the landing at once, Henry. Tell them to hurry."

Then, while Henry was flashing his message into the night, Captain Hardy ran to the window to see what the *Patrol* would do. On and on it went, as though it had no intention of stopping, and cold beads of perspiration stood out on Captain Hardy's forehead, and he clasped and unclasped his hands in his excitement. On went the boat. Captain Hardy tore back to Henry's side.

"What do they say?" he demanded.

"They're coming, sir."

Again the captain stepped to the window. The little steamer was just beginning to turn.

"Get your hats and coats, quick," ordered the leader.

In a second the scouts were ready. In another, the little party emerged from the house and started pell-mell down the hill in a mad race to reach the landing before the police-boat got there.

Lewis E. Theiss

Boat and boys touched the wharf at almost the same instant, and Captain Hardy's party leaped aboard before the steamer had entirely lost her headway. An officer stood at the gunwale, peering through the dark at the figures that swarmed aboard.

"I'm Lieutenant Gavigan, in command," he said, advancing toward Captain Hardy. "Are you the party that called us?"

"Yes," replied Captain Hardy.

A look of astonishment came over the lieutenant's face. "Your wireless said we was wanted by the secret service," said the puzzled lieutenant, "but these boys do not belong to the secret service. And I don't know you, either."

"I will explain everything," said Captain Hardy, "but make haste. We're after German spies that are to meet at Hell Gate at nine o'clock. Crowd on every ounce of steam you can."

"Hell Gate!" said the lieutenant sarcastically. "And do you think I'm going to take you to Hell Gate, just on your say-so—you and a crowd of kids I don't know from Adam? What do you think would happen to Lieutenant Gavigan if he went gallivantin' round the Bay without orders on joy rides like that? Nothin' doin'."

Captain Hardy smothered the indignation he felt, and began to explain courteously. "Lieutenant Gavigan," he said, "I am Captain Hardy of the United States Medical Reserve Corps and these boys are members of the Camp Brady Wireless Patrol. Last summer we did the wireless work for some of the Pennsylvania troops guarding public works, and in the course of our duties were fortunate enough to detect and capture some German spies who were endeavoring to blow up a great reservoir and cause another flood like that which wiped out Johnstown. For the last few weeks we have been helping the United States secret service keep track of German spies in New York, for, as you no doubt know, the secret service is short handed."

"Short handed," sneered the lieutenant. "Yes, and short minded, too, to be employin' a parcel of kids. But that's about as much sense as the secret service has got. If they want any spies caught, why don't they call in the cops? We'd catch 'em soon enough."

Captain Hardy choked down his resentment and went on. "We're not making any boasts as to our abilities, Lieutenant Gavigan," he said, "but we are doing all we can to help and the secret service thought well enough of us to put us to work."

The police officer looked the captain over critically. "How do I know you are what you say you are?" he asked. "Where are your credentials?"

A sudden fear smote Captain Hardy. Were all their efforts to come to naught? Were the treacherous spies to get away, now, when it seemed that they might yet be apprehended?

"We have never thought credentials would be necessary," he said, "and we have overlooked the need of providing ourselves with them. But we can satisfy you fully. Only hurry, Lieutenant, hurry."

"And where should I hurry?" the latter asked truculently. "You don't think I'm goin' to risk my head takin' the likes of you on a joy ride to Hell Gate, do you? Nothin' doin'. You come ashore and tell the captain who you are and what you want, and if he says Hell Gate, why, you'll get there, and if he don't, you won't. And that's all there is to that."

Lewis E. Theiss

Very evidently it was useless to argue with the stubborn lieutenant. In despair Captain Hardy turned aside, desperately thinking how to meet the situation. Argument, he saw, was of no avail with this type of man. Force would have to be used. But what had he to offer that would impress the man?

"Captain Hardy," said Roy, slipping up to his commander, "would our police cards help any?"

"The very thing," said Captain Hardy "I had forgotten that you boys had them."

Captain Hardy hastened back to the commander of the Patrol. "Lieutenant Gavigan," he said sharply, "there are more ways than one a policeman can lose his head. One is by being a fool. Your Commissioner is keenly interested in this work of ours and is giving us all the assistance he can. Each one of my boys carries his personal permission to go where he chooses. Roy, show this officer your pass."

Roy produced his police card, and the three other boys followed his example.

"Those cards were given to my boys by the Commissioner in person," said Captain Hardy impressively. "He is keeping in close touch with this work. I should not want to have to report that you blocked our efforts and made it possible for these spies to escape."

The change in Lieutenant Gavigan was remarkable. "Crowd on all the steam you've got, Jim," he shouted to the engineer. Then turning to Captain Hardy, he said, "Why didn't you tell me you was on police business? I'll send a wireless message at once for instructions."

Captain Hardy raised his hand in protest. "Impossible!" he said. "If the Germans should pick it up, everything would be lost. Our success depends wholly upon the speed and secrecy with which we travel. How much longer will it take to reach Hell Gate?"

"A half an hour, anyway," said the lieutenant, who was beginning to look worried. Then he added, "I'm takin' an awful chance, goin' up there without orders."

"And you're taking a worse one if you refuse to go," rejoined Captain Hardy sternly.

The lieutenant wavered. Captain Hardy strode into the cabin and seized a piece of paper. Lieutenant Gavigan, curious, followed him. Rapidly Captain Hardy wrote a message on the paper.

"Send that to your Commissioner," he said, handing the completed message to the commander of the *Patrol*.

Lieutenant Gavigan ran his eyes hurriedly over the paper. "Captain James Hardy, M. R. C.," ran the message, "and patrol of boys request immediate assistance. Everything at stake. Send instructions at once."

The lieutenant looked relieved. "The Commissioner won't be at his office at this hour," he said, "but they'll know where to reach him."

"Then rush it," said Captain Hardy, "and make every bit of speed you can."

He stepped out into the night again. Overhead myriad stars twinkled brightly. The little craft was vibrating from stem to stern under the rapid revolution of her engines. She was ploughing through the water, throwing up a great white wave on either bow. On all sides of her vessels were coming and going on their usual missions of peaceful industry. Millions of lights twinkled in the great buildings of the city and in the factories that lined the water-front. But Captain Hardy had no eye for the beauties of the night or the swelling waves or the stimulating harbor scene. He could think of nothing but the work ahead of him, of the rendezvous in the darkness at Hell Gate. The little steamer, ploughing her way through the water, seemed to Captain Hardy to be almost motionless, so keen were his fears that he would be too late. He pulled out his watch and groaned. The boat was well into the East River, but it was already almost nine o'clock. In agony of mind he began to pace up and down the deck.

"Got an answer," said Lieutenant Gavigan, suddenly coming out of the cabin, and he thrust a paper into Captain Hardy's hand.

The latter stepped toward the light and read it. "Give any assistance requested," it read. "Thank goodness, that's settled," muttered Captain Hardy.

Then he turned to the lieutenant, who was now more than ready to oblige. "Can't you get a little more speed out of her?" he demanded.

"I'll try," said the boat's commander, and he strode off to the engine room.

Past the Brooklyn Bridge, past the Manhattan Bridge, past the Navy Yard, past factories and offices and great rows of tenements, the little police-boat sped on. But the hands of Captain Hardy's watch sped faster. Past Blackwell's Island, with its long prison buildings, past the little lighthouse at its northern end, past the darkened area of the East River Park, on toward the blackness of Hell Gate with its frightful swirling waters, rushed the speeding craft. And now, drawn by a common interest, boys and men alike crowded the bow, and policemen and scouts stood in a close knot, gazing eagerly ahead into the darkness.

A motor-boat suddenly shot across the path of the Patrol. "Halt!" cried Lieutenant Gavigan, seizing a megaphone. The motor-boat came to. Lieutenant Gavigan was about to stop to examine it.

"Go on," said Captain Hardy tensely. "That's not the boat—and there's only one man in it anyway. We're after a gang."

Darker became the way. The river broadened. The waters grew troubled. High above loomed the great arch of the new railroad bridge over Hell Gate. A sailing craft drifted silently toward them. Lieutenant Gavigan looked questioningly toward Captain Hardy. The latter shook his head.

Again he drew forth his watch and held it close to his face. "Nine ten," he said, in a voice that shook with emotion.

On rushed the little steamer. It began to turn its nose toward the wicked waters that gave the region its name. Then it ploughed into the swirls and headed for the smooth reaches beyond. No craft of any sort could be seen.

"We'll have to go through," said the lieutenant. "We can't turn here."

The boat passed under the great bridge and on through the seething rapids. It ran on for a little distance, then circled and swung back. Again it passed through the angry waters, then made a wide circuit, steaming slowly along the land, while those aboard searched the darkness, peering into every curve and indentation of the shore, to try to spy out some sign of life. Tugs were shunting car barges, and an occasional steam craft passed, but nowhere was there a sign of a motor-boat or of the fugitive Germans.

A great doubt came into Captain Hardy's mind. Could it be that after all they had been on a wild-goose chase? He had thought the connection between Hell Gate and the Balaklavan rendezvous far-fetched. But it had been the one chance left. They had tried the theory out and they were wrong. The wireless patrol had not merely lost the Germans. They had lost all trace of them. They had failed in the crisis.

CHAPTER XX

A CLUE FROM THE AIR

Slowly the little police-boat finished her circuit, nosing into every dark nook and spying out every black corner; but blacker than either the night or the water was the gloom in the hearts of Captain Hardy and his fellow members of the wireless patrol. With bowed head the disappointed leader turned to the commander of the boat, to tell him to return to his dock. But Captain Hardy was too loyal to his fellows, too resentful of Lieutenant Gavigan's remarks about them to indicate by word or act that he thought they had been on a wild-goose chase. So he said simply, "We were too late, Lieutenant. They have given us the slip. But none the less I thank you for your assistance."

Then he turned aside and stood peering gloomily into the dark waters, that reflected the exact shade of his own mind. Appreciating better than his youthful companions the full extent of the disaster that had befallen them, he could not, for the time being, summon up his usual fortitude or see any hopeful prospect. Now that the spies knew that they were discovered, he felt sure that they would never risk the sending of another wireless message. And a wireless message was the sole clue by which his little patrol might once more pick up the trail of the fugitives.

Lewis E. Theiss

But Captain Hardy's disappointment was no whit keener than that of his fellows, nor his sufferings any more poignant; yet with the buoyancy of inexperienced youth, hope was not entirely crushed in the heart of any one of the young scouts. So absolute was their faith in their leader, so astonishing had been the good fortune that so far had attended their efforts, that each felt that in some way this present disaster would yet be retrieved. And with hope as a motive power, each began, in a manner true to his character, to attack the problem that confronted them, to get ready for further service. It was a splendid example of the spirit of "never say die" that their leader had drilled into them—an example that he would be quick to follow, once the shock of disappointment had passed away.

Lew, hopeless of solving the puzzle of the spies' disappearance, was thinking of how the scouts should equip themselves if they should be called upon for a land pursuit; for at following trails and taking care of himself in the open he had no superior in the wireless patrol. Roy, keen minded as a Sherlock Holmes, was turning over in his mind the problem of the spies' escape, trying to reason out what their line of action would be in the immediate future. Willie was examining a mental landscape to decide the same question. With that wonderful facility of memory he had acquired by hours of practice at Camp Brady, he now called up the maps of the neighboring waters he had been studying; and in his mind's eye he could see every point and indentation of the shore-lines, every arm of water, every inequality of the land as pictured on the contour map, and the principal roads of the region. And he was asking himself what a party of fugitives in a small boat would naturally do.

Henry, eager as always to learn more about the wireless, had ingratiated himself with the *Patrol's* wireless man and was eagerly examining his instruments and plying him with questions. At first the operator answered with good-natured tolerance as one replies to the queries of a child. But when he saw how much Henry actually knew, and found that though he was only a boy he had already acted as operator at a government wireless station, he fell into an earnest discussion about the possibilities of wireless in police work—for in New York the police wireless was still in an experimental stage. Then he permitted Henry to clamp on the receivers and listen in.

Henry welcomed the opportunity, for in all the weeks they had been watching the Germans, the wireless patrol had hardly had an opportunity to listen to the myriad voices in the air. They had had to shut out all other sounds and tune down to the low lengths used by the Germans—and by nobody else. They had been like spectators at the opera with their ears plugged to shut out the music.

Now, as Henry eagerly listened in, he caught a sharp, whining note that vibrated powerfully in his ear. "There's the Navy Yard calling," he said, and a deep frown passed over his face, for it made him think of submarines and the failure of the wireless patrol. For a moment he tuned to a short length and listened for a spy message, as he had done so many times before.

"That's the Waldorf-Astoria talking," said Henry a moment later, and he copied down the message and shoved it over to the police operator.

Then followed press despatches—stories of land and sea, of fires and battles, of shipwrecks and the arrest of a spy. And again Henry scowled and slid his tuning-coil and briefly listened in at lower range.

Down the river ploughed the little steamer, repassing, one by

Lewis E. Theiss

one, the landmarks it had passed on its trip northward. As it steamed along and the meaning of their failure became more apparent to the young scouts, they became gloomier and gloomier. But Henry, exulting at the opportunity to handle such an outfit, almost forgot their failure, and drank in eagerly the gossip of the night. So engrossed was he, that he was startled when he heard the order to slacken speed, and heard his captain say, "Well, here we are, boys."

Reluctantly he removed the receivers. Then, as an after-thought struck him, he clamped them again to his ears, tuned his coil to a low length, and strained his ears in one last search for a forbidden voice in the dark. For a moment he sat listening vainly. Then, with unwilling fingers, he began to take the clamps from his head. But suddenly he jammed the receivers back on his ears and sat tense.

"Hurry up, Henry," called Captain Hardy. "We're waiting for you."

"Hush!" said Henry, lifting a warning hand. Then he sat rigid, bending eagerly forward. In his ear a call was sounding. It was the old familiar call of the motor station. He seized a pencil and began to write. A moment later he jumped to his feet and went rushing after his captain.

"Here!" he called, thrusting a paper into Captain Hardy's hand. "The motor-car station just sent this message."

"The motor-car station!" exclaimed Captain Hardy, in astonishment. "Then Sanders can't be aboard the motor-boat. The Chief said he had him covered so closely that he could not escape—and evidently he couldn't." A moment later Captain Hardy stood frowning, trying to puzzle out the meaning of it. "I don't see how he could have sent a message," he continued, "if he is so closely watched that he couldn't get away."

"Perhaps the message will tell us," suggested Roy.

"Right again, Roy," said Captain Hardy. "We'll hurry to the office and decipher it."

On the run they made their way to the subway station at Bowling Green. They caught a north bound train and shortly afterward swarmed up out of the subway and made a rush for the secret service offices.

With hardly more than a word of greeting they drew up at a table and laid the paper with the message before them.

"Forty," said Captain Hardy, counting the letters. "If they use the same cipher they did last time, that'll make five columns of eight letters each." Rapidly he set down the letters in the order indicated, thus:

```
T T E N R
H A S E Y
G Y U R A
I L O E B
N T V R O
D C Z E H
I A E V C
M X D E E
```

Then slowly he read off the message: "ECHO—BAY—REVERE—RENDEZVOUS—EXACTLY—AT—MIDNIGHT."

With a cry of joy Captain Hardy leaped to his feet. "We've got another chance," he said. "Sanders must be going to meet them at Revere Rendezvous—wherever that is." Then, turning to a man at the next desk, he inquired, "Where is Echo Bay?"

"At New Rochelle," said the agent. "That's where Fort Slocum is."

"Fort Slocum!" cried Captain Hardy. "This may be even more serious than it seems. Can this man be spying on the fort, too? How far is New Rochelle from here?"

"Eighteen or twenty miles."

"Can we get there by twelve o'clock?"

"Sure. Why?"

"The spies we are after are to meet at Echo Bay, Revere Rendezvous, at midnight. Are you sure that we can get there?" Then he glanced at his watch. "It's already long past ten."

The Chief was still at the office. The agent went to consult him, and came back for details. Captain Hardy stepped into the Chief's private office and made the entire situation plain. The Chief sat like a cake of ice, a thinking machine immovable and unmoved, listening to the recital.

"How many men have you here?" he asked his subordinate, the instant Captain Hardy had done talking.

"Four."

"Two of you go by automobile, two by motorboat. Divide these boys and take half with each party. Let those who go by land approach the meeting-place on foot and hide. The motorboat must come in behind the spy boat and cut off retreat. Be sure you are armed."

Lewis E. Theiss

CHAPTER XXI

THE CAPTURE OF THE SPIES

Without a moment's delay the party that was to go by boat, including Henry and Roy, rushed off to the dock where the secret service had a motor craft of the racing type, capable of making tremendous speed. Almost as quickly the other party found itself seated in a powerful touring-car, speeding northward. Captain Hardy, Willie, and Lew were in the car, together with the two agents and the driver, who was likewise a secret service man.

Up Third Avenue rolled the big automobile, dodging wagons, shooting past motor-cars, darting by trolleys, its horn shrieking an almost unceasing warning as it charged onward at the very top of the speed limit. Never had Willie or Lew ridden so fast in crowded thoroughfares, and time and again they held their breath as the big car rushed toward some obstacle in its path, expecting a crash. But under the skilled hands of the driver the great machine swept in and out, weaving its way through the traffic as an eel glides through water growths.

The first thrill passed, they turned to their captain and the secret service agents who were earnestly discussing the situation. Overhead the thunder of the elevated trains was such that at times they could hardly hear what the men beside them were saying.

"I am well acquainted with New Rochelle and the region of Echo Bay," said one of the agents, "but I never heard of any Revere Rendezvous there. However, the people of the town can doubtless tell us. We shall have time to make inquiries." And turning to the driver, he said, "Shove her to the limit, Jim."

Already the car was well up-town. Traffic had grown steadily less, and as steadily the driver increased his speed. Now they were rolling over the smooth asphalt at twenty miles an hour.

"No doubt they could tell us," replied Captain Hardy, "if there were any such place. But I fear that the name is one of the spies' own making," and he told the story of the Balaklavan rendezvous. "We think that meant Hell Gate," explained Captain Hardy. "The fact that the spies' motor-boat is now evidently on the Sound confirms that belief. But the name was far-fetched. It took us a long time to work it out. This new name may be equally obscure. We shall have to decipher it on the way."

The motor-car was approaching the Harlem River. "Your Balaklavan rendezvous is only a few blocks off there," said the agent, pointing to the east.

The car rolled up to the bridge and passed over the dark waters where tugs were shunting car-floats into their docks and churning up white foam with their propellers. Thousands of lights were reflected in the black depths. In a moment the Harlem was behind them, and they were in the borough of the Bronx. On they sped up Third Avenue.

Lewis E. Theiss

The two boys were distracted. They wanted to see the sights, utterly new to them, and they wanted to hear the discussion of their elders. Willie, with that strange faculty of his for noting places and locations, kept watching the street signs and trying to remember where Third Avenue led to on the map.

"There are three places on Echo Bay where a motor-boat and a motor-car can easily meet," said one of the secret service men. "At the north side of the harbor entrance is a finger of land called Premium Point. On the other shore is Huguenot Park. And an arm of the bay runs inland all the way to the main street passing north through the town."

"Which place would they be most likely to select?" asked Captain Hardy.

"Well, they'd hardly try Premium Point because that is a private estate, and they would have difficulty in getting to the water-front."

"Then that limits them to the two others."

"Exactly. And one is as easy to get to as the other."

Captain Hardy frowned. "What are we going to do?" he asked. "We might pick the wrong place and miss them. And since there are several of these spies in the boat, and they are desperate fellows, we'd never dare divide our forces. What are we going to do?"

"Gee!" said Willie. "We just passed Two Hundredth Street. Some town, eh, with two hundred numbered streets?"

The car rushed on. In silence the three men were considering how they should meet the situation before them.

"If only we could get into touch with our motor-boat," said one of the secret service men, "we could arrange a plan to cover every possibility."

"We've got to find what this Revere Rendezvous is," insisted Captain Hardy. "Can't you think of anything that would suggest such a name?"

The three men fell silent, pondering the matter. The car swept on.

"Hello!" said Willie. "We've left Third Avenue, but we're going so fast now I can't make out the names on the sign-posts."

And indeed they were going. As they approached the edge of the city limits, where there was little traffic and the driver could see far ahead, he pressed his foot on the accelerator and the great car went roaring through the street at more than thirty miles an hour. And as they drew closer and closer to the open country, the man at the wheel rushed them on faster and faster. In vain Willie looked at the sign-posts. The car darted past them with baffling speed. But Willie wanted to know where he was.

"What street are we on now?" he asked, leaning toward the driver.

"The Boston Post Road," said the driver, without turning his head.

Captain Hardy caught the name and his eyes flashed. "The Boston Post Road!" he repeated. "Does this go anywhere near New Rochelle?"

"Right through it," said the driver, "only they call it Main

Street within the town limits."

"Does it pass near Echo Bay?"

"It's the very road that meets the arm of the bay."

Captain Hardy turned from the driver to the other secret service men. "Can you think of anything that would connect the name of Revere with the point where the bay touches this road?"

"By George!" cried one of the men. "You've hit it exactly. I had forgotten all about it, but there's a stone marker in a wee bit of a park, put up to commemorate the passage of Paul Revere on his famous ride. He came down this very road, and that marker is almost at the exact spot where the road touches the arm of the bay."

"Good!" said the captain. "That is probably the place."

"Beyond a doubt. It's the logical place, too, come to think of it. For if a fellow drove into Huguenot Park and found that somebody was trailing him, he couldn't get away. He'd be bottled up. But if he stuck to the Boston Post Road, he'd have all New England to run to. What's more, there's a road-house near by, where cars can be left. Things couldn't have been made to order any better."

"Then I guess our course is clear," said the other agent. "We'll leave our car near by and find good hiding-places close to the water at this point."

Meantime, the motor-boat, breasting the waves as though striving for a speed prize, had borne Henry and Roy and their older companions rapidly back over the path they had so recently traversed. Up the East River the craft went roaring, under the great bridges, that at night seemed only strings of fairy lights arching the stream, past prison walls and towering tenements, and on to the swirling rapids so recently visited.

The two boys paid little attention to what they were passing. Already they had seen it twice. But never had either of them seen a craft like that they were in. It was one of those long, low racing boats, steered with a wheel like a motor-car, and slopingly decked over in front to shield the driver. And it roared like an aeroplane as it tore through the water. For the boys in the boat were rushing toward their goal almost as swiftly as their comrades on land.

What most interested Henry and Roy was the array of buttons and knobs and other instruments on the dashboard, like the lighting buttons and speedometer on an automobile.

"I wonder what they are for," said Roy to Henry. "I never saw a boat like this before."

"Nor I, either," replied Henry.

"Right you are," said one of their companions. "There probably isn't another like it. It's both a motor-boat and an electric boat. Sometimes we have to be very quiet about our work and then we would never dare go roaring along as we are now. You can hear us a mile away. So we have an electric motor and storage batteries for quiet work. When we run by electricity, we don't make any more noise than a swan."

The boys expressed their admiration. "And nobody could see you, either," said Roy. "The boat's exactly the color of the water. When it's as dark as this, I'll bet you couldn't see it fifty yards away."

Lewis E. Theiss

"Well, you may have a chance to test your belief," said the agent with a smile.

"What do you think will happen?" asked Roy.

"I don't know. But when that German motor-boat goes into Echo Bay, we've got to go after it; and we don't dare be seen, either."

"What's the bay like?" inquired Henry.

"It's an irregular little sheet of water with several small islands in it; and if these Germans go clear in, we'll nab them easily. But if they don't, we may have a lively chase."

On rushed the motor-boat. Past Classon Point, past the long projecting finger of land known as Throgs Neck, with Fort Schuyler at its extremity, then northward again into ever widening waters, past Elm Point, and Hewlett Point, and Barker Point until they were fairly in the wider reaches of Long Island Sound.

On the right loomed the high and precipitous shores of Long Island, hardly visible in the cloudy darkness. On the left, far across the waving waters, was the unseen ragged coast of the mainland, broken by a hundred irregular indentations, studded with numberless little promontories, and fringed with islands as a woman's throat is girt with a necklace of beads. Ahead of them stretched untold miles of gently heaving water. And there, too, blazed two beacons to point the path for mariners—the Sands Point Light, topping the eastern bluff, and the fiery eye of Execution Rocks, that reared their jagged pinnacles far out from the shore, to tear the bottoms of unwary ships.

"We'll go straight north," said the man at the wheel, "for

those spies are without doubt biding their time in some sheltering cove among the islands over there. And there they will doubtless stay until the hour to meet their comrade."

He flashed a pocket torch on his watch. "We are in good time," he said. "We shall get there well before them. Then we shall have to hide and see what happens."

Straight up the Sound drove the rushing racer, plunging through the rolling swells, tossing the spray to right and left. Ahead of it glowed and winked the fiery eyes of the lighthouses. Along either shore shone innumerable street lamps and the lights of late retiring householders. Save for themselves the water seemed deserted. The great steamers that ply between New England and the metropolis had long since passed and vanished in the misty darkness to the north. No freighters were breasting the waves, no tugs were puffing along with strings of barges in their rear. No ferry-boats were crossing. And none of the legion of sailing craft and motor-boats, none of the thousands of pleasure yachts that sometimes dot the smiling waters in the daytime, was abroad. The little secret-service boat seemed to be alone in that vast expanse of water.

Suddenly the boat careened violently. The boys were alarmed, but their comrades merely smiled.

"We're turning," explained the man at the wheel. "Now we'll go straight into the harbor. And it will be just as well if we make less noise."

He slowed down his engine and the roaring sound died away. The boat fell off in speed, but still pushed ahead with good momentum. For perhaps a mile the boat advanced. Then the driver shut off his engine entirely.

"Those fellows might be in Echo Bay itself," he said. "They couldn't find a safer place to hide than right among the pleasure craft. We won't take any chance of being discovered. We'll just glide in like a shadow and anchor where we can watch things."

He switched over to his electric drive and the boat began to forge ahead again, but with all the stealth of a tiger in the jungle. The operation of its machinery was noiseless, and only the gentle slap of the waves against the bow gave audible evidence of its passage. For a considerable time they rode in silence. In the thick darkness the shore was almost invisible while the glowing street lights that shone here and there served only to accentuate the blackness of the night. Close together in the cockpit huddled the passengers, for the air was raw and chilly.

"Until we've got those fellows safe in handcuffs," said the man in charge of the party, "I don't want one of you to speak aloud. And stay down in the bottom of the boat where you can't be seen."

Noticeably the speed of the little craft fell off, It no longer drove through the waves, but slipped through them so softly that even the gentle splashing at the bow was ended. Presently Henry missed the slight vibration, of which he had been but semi-conscious, and he knew that the pilot had shut off his power completely.

Now the shores, with their towering trees, began to loom up uncertainly in the darkness, and Henry knew that the boat was slipping into the harbor. Presently he became aware of a dark spot ahead of them on the water, then another, and another; and straining his eyes, he saw that before them lay a great company of motor-boats and sailing yachts. Very slowly his own craft drew nearer, for it had all but lost its headway, until it was close to the fleet of pleasure boats. Then there was a tiny splash and one of the secret service men began to pay out the anchor rope over the side. The little boat came to rest, and lay quiet, rolling gently, while its occupants crouched in the cockpit, listening and peering through the thick darkness as they waited.

Never had either of the boys been in such a situation before, and the strangeness, the mysteriousness of it impressed them powerfully. All the sights and sounds of the day were missing and in their place arose a host of unfamiliar sensations. Mist was rising all about them, making the darkness denser and more impenetrable. Not a star was to be seen. The shore-line was only a vague, uncertain black bulk. As they huddled silently in the bottom of the little boat, they became conscious of the voices of the night; but these voices were different from the nocturnal whisperings of field and forest which they knew so well. Now they heard only the lisping of water. Little wavelets broke gently against their slender craft. And all about them rose the musical whisper, the liquid murmur of waters gently lapping the rocks or swelling against the sides of boats. At times the breeze could be heard sighing softly through the rigging of near-by yachts. It was weird and uncanny.

And the sensations that came of it were strange and powerful. In the forest the young scouts had lain in wait for enemies, had hidden in the darkness to trap desperate foes, had watched, with bated breath and pounding hearts, for shadowy forms to appear. They were not unaccustomed to danger and the suspense of an ambush. But in the forest they had solid ground beneath their feet. Trees and other tangible objects were all about them. But here everything seemed unreal, almost ghostly. The darkness of the forest was no blacker than the night here in the open. And yet there was no shady covering of leaves to shut out the light—only a strange, weird, unearthly canopy of mist. In the forest innumerable tree trunks offered concealment to approaching enemies; yet here in the open with nothing tangible to obstruct the vision, it was almost impossible to see anything, strain the eyes as one might.

A feeling of awe came over the young scouts, and both were conscious of a creepy sensation. So unreal appeared their surroundings that it seemed as though anything coming out of the mist would be kin to it, unreal and ghostly. So they sat in the bottom of the boat, only the tops of their heads showing above the low gunwale, as they waited in breathless silence, peering through the night, listening with cocked ear, and straining forward to catch every slightest sound.

Under the covered bow of the boat, the driver flashed his torch for a second on the face of his watch.

"Eleven forty-five," he muttered. "There ought to be something doing soon."

A minute passed. The silence was unbroken. Another minute went by. The sighing of the wind in near-by riggings was the only audible sound. Again a minute passed. No sound of boat or boatmen broke the gloomy silence. Once more the pilot peeped stealthily at his watch and gave a muttered exclamation. A feeling of uneasiness took possession of the watchers. They stirred nervously. Dark fears crept into their minds. Had something happened to alter the plans of the spies? Had Sanders sent another wireless message to his comrades, naming another meeting-place? Henry's heart almost stopped beating at the thought that it might well have happened. Bending toward his comrade, he whispered his fears. His voice trembled as he spoke. Roy uttered a low exclamation of dismay. Then there was silence again, and the four sat listening with strained attention—listening for what they feared they would never hear.

And then they heard it. From far down the Sound came the reports of a rapidly beating marine motor. At first the noise was so faint as scarcely to be audible, like the dropping of a pin on a bare floor. Then the fog seemed to magnify the sound and it became suddenly louder. Then it died away again, but it was more distinct than it had been at first. A minute passed. Noticeably the sound grew in volume. Another minute passed. Distinct now was every beat of the motor. With lips parted, heads slightly turned, and eyes peering through the dark, the watchers waited with beating pulses as the sound came on. There could be no doubt it was made by a fast craft. And there could be no doubt that the boat was rushing northward close to the shore. Was it the boat they waited for? Would it turn at the harbor entrance? Or would it go tearing onward, leaving them in despair?

Now it was almost abreast of the harbor's mouth. Another minute, a few seconds, would tell the story. And not one of the watchers breathed as they hung on the sound. On and on it came, until the scouts knew that it was directly abreast of the channel. Would it turn? Would it enter the harbor? Or would it rush straight by? Unable longer to control himself, Roy stretched out his hand and gripped Henry's shoulder. And Henry, like himself, was all atremble. The secret service men stirred nervously. But nobody said a word.

Then the passage of the sound seemed to end. It was no longer rushing by. It seemed stationary. But momentarily it grew in volume. It was coming straight toward the watchers. The boat had entered the harbor. A sigh of relief escaped every lip.

"Up with your anchor," whispered the pilot, "before he shuts off his power."

His companion leaned stealthily over the side and rapidly paid in the rope, lifting the light anchor over the gunwale and cautiously stowing it in the bottom. And he was none too soon. Hardly was the anchor aboard before the roaring sound ceased and the oncoming boat approached with lessened speed. But the scouts' boat rode free, ready for instant work.

"Down with you," whispered the pilot. "Keep your heads below the gunwale till they're past."

The party crouched lower. On came the spy boat. Its muffled engine beats were hardly louder than the pounding of the hearts that watched. It drove steadily forward. Now it was a few fathoms astern. Now it was abreast. Now it had passed. Stealthily four heads slipped above the gunwale of the scout boat. The spy craft was already lost in darkness. The pilot grasped his wheel. He turned a switch and the boat began to vibrate silently. Then it moved forward, gathering momentum with every second. Under the covered deck the other agent flashed a light on his watch.

"Eleven fifty-eight," he whispered. "They figured it down close."

On went the boat. The craft ahead of them was still invisible though but a few hundred feet distant. But by peering sharply at the water, the pilot could see where it had passed. The surface was still agitated. Faintly came the sound of the muffled motor. The pilot increased his speed, but no sound came from his boat. Like a ghost it glided through the dark waters.

"Look sharp," whispered the pilot. "Let me know if you see them. We've got to get as close to them as we can, and yet we must not be seen."

On went the spy craft. It slid past the park. The street leading to that was faintly illumined by occasional lights.

The pilot uttered a low exclamation of alarm. "If they look back," he whispered, "those lights will betray us. We're right between them and the spies."

Sharply he swung his craft to the right, crowding close to the shallow waters that edged the channel. If he ran into the mud flats disaster might result. But to stay where they would be silhouetted against the street lights was to court discovery. He had chosen the lesser of two evils.

On they went. Not yet had they come in sight of the fugitive craft in front of them. The pilot increased his speed, leaning anxiously forward as he peered through the darkness. Over the sides of the boat his fellows craned their necks, searching the blackness for a glimpse of the quarry.

Suddenly they became aware that the motor ahead of them had stopped. Then masses of shadow seemed to close in on either hand, making the water itself darker than ever. The boat ahead had turned off its power and was propelled only by the momentum it had gained. Instinctively Roy laid his hand on the pilot's shoulder. But the latter had already stopped his engine.

As silent as a shadow the boat slid forward. Suddenly Roy detected what he was looking for. At the same moment a high bank loomed up directly before them. The craft ahead turned toward the right and slipped along the narrowing channel. A few yards further on, it came to rest, its nose lying softly against the muddy shore. Before it the steep bank led upward to an open, level space that both Roy and Henry felt instinctively was a public highway; for on either hand, though at many rods' distance, could be seen the glow of a lamp that was invisible itself.

The scout boat also came to rest, its momentum overcome by the resistance of the water. Like a shadow it lay, not more than fifty yards from the waiting spy craft. Crouching low behind the gunwale, its four occupants held their breath as they watched the party in the boat ahead. Assisted by the faint glow of the distant street lamps, they could vaguely make out the forms of their quarry; while the darkness of their own background rendered them practically invisible.

But no one in the spy boat was looking behind him. All were straining their eyes for the man they had come to meet. Excepting for the gentle voices of the night there was not a sound. Then a whistle rose from the spy boat—a short, sharp note thrice repeated. From the darkness an answer sounded a dozen rods distant. Then footsteps were heard, as some one picked his way uncertainly along the sloping bank. Suddenly the footsteps ceased and stillness reigned. Roy instantly comprehended the fact that the person approaching had paused to listen. His heart gave a leap of joy. He himself had heard no alarming noises, but he instantly guessed that something had caught the ear of the stranger. And Roy knew that his companions who had come by motor-car must have made these sounds. Trembling with excitement, he gripped Henry's shoulder.

On came the man. Now the scouts could vaguely distinguish his form. He called in a low voice, and some one in the spy boat answered. Suddenly the man turned sharp about. From the darkness behind him came the unmistakable sound of a pebble kicked by a human foot. In the opposite direction a stone rolled down the bank and splashed noisily into the water. With an oath, the man on the bank turned and ran toward the motor-boat. To right and left in the darkness came the scurrying of feet and the command "Halt!" The fugitive leaped forward. Frantically the men in the spy craft were trying to head their boat about. The fugitive reached it and leaped aboard. Then he turned to face the figures rushing toward him. At the same instant the scout boat suddenly moved forward. From the spy boat a pistol-shot rang out. Before another could follow, an electric torch was shining full on the spy craft, and the agent in the scout boat was covering the fugitives with his automatic.

"Drop that gun!" he commanded. "Hands up, or I'll fire!"

Taken by surprise, the man who had just boarded the craft let his weapon clatter to the floor. And in the sudden illumination Henry saw with exultation that the man was the motor-car driver, the German agent, Sanders.

"Hands up!" repeated the secret service man imperatively, noticing that one of the fugitives was crouching in the bottom of the boat with his hands hidden. In reply the man straightened up. Like a flash his arm shot out and a pistol cracked. But before a second bullet could follow, a form leaped into the shallow water and a great fist shot into the man's stomach, doubling him up like a jack-knife. The same hand then grasped the nose of the spy craft and dragged it toward the shore, while the pilot of the scout boat brought his craft close beside that of the spies. Other torches flashed in the darkness, and one by one the fugitives were manacled—Sanders, and the spy from the cliff, and the German grocer, and his errand boy, and a stranger who ran the boat.

CHAPTER XXII

A TASK ACCOMPLISHED

Two hours later the party was grouped around Chief Flynn, who had remained in his office to learn the result of the raid. Both motor-boats had been left in charge of the New Rochelle road-house keeper, and the entire party had returned to New York in the two motor-cars—the secret service motor and Sanders' car, for Sanders had left it at the road-house and slipped away into the darkness at midnight. The clerk from Hoboken was under arrest, too. He had been taken up by the man who was watching him. Sanders had eluded his shadow by leaving his car late in the afternoon, at a garage, ostensibly to have it washed, and by later leaving his house surreptitiously in the dark. He had not been able to reach the Balaklavan rendezvous in time to join his companions. But they had a wireless equipment aboard their boat and he had made a later appointment with them. And, even as Captain Hardy had suspected, he had been nosing around Fort Slocum in the darkness.

But this was all the secret service ever learned as to the operations of this gang of wireless spies. The prisoners refused to name those higher up, and the Chief could only guess whose might be the master minds behind the plot.

As for the various wireless agents who were relaying the spy messages to Mexico, several were caught by decoy messages and shared the fate of Sanders and the others.

Even the mystery of the sudden flight of Sanders and his crew was cleared up. Following the Chief's orders, his men on the border had taken the three silver coins away from the Mexican. And, sure enough, the coins contained messages. One was the message from New York concerning the sailing of transports. The other messages were about army secrets, and it is not yet known where they came from or how they got into the hands of the Mexican.

The latter protested violently when asked for his silver dollars, and they had to be taken from him by force. The next day one of his guards discovered that the left cuff of his shirt was missing. The shirt had been intact when he was arrested. No trace of the cuff could be found anywhere. The window of the room where the Mexican was confined overlooked a public street. And it was believed by the secret service men that the spy had written a message on his cuff in some way and dropped it out of the window to a confederate. Thereupon a warning had been flashed back along the wireless line—a warning message in the new cipher that had so puzzled the lads of the wireless patrol.

"It's all clear enough now," sighed Willie, when the story had been put together, "but when you have only one piece of a jig-saw puzzle you can't make much out of it. And one piece was about all we had for a long time. I see it all now, but there's one thing I don't yet understand. Why didn't they use a more difficult cipher?"

"I suppose," explained the Chief, "that this very pursuit and capture of the spies answers that question. They knew that if the secret service picked up their messages, we could sooner or later decipher anything they sent. But even a very simple cipher might baffle one unaccustomed to such things. Always there was the danger that some one would pick up their messages. So they chose ciphers that would bother the ordinary man but that they themselves could read readily. They didn't dare use a cipher that would require a long time to unravel, because they foresaw that they might have to flee on short notice, just as it happened."

"I see," said Willie.

"And now," said the Chief, "I want to tell you boys and your good leader here how much you have done for me and your country. I didn't have faith in your accomplishing much, but I thought that you might be able to pick up wireless messages, if any were abroad, and so I agreed to take you. You see we were almost desperate over the situation. We knew what was going on, but we were so terribly short handed that we could not spare men to run the spies down. I think that we shall have no more trouble. The system is broken up. If we do have trouble, I'm going to send for you boys at once. Meantime, you can now go back home, knowing that few boys have done as much for America and Freedom as you. I am more grateful to you than I can tell you."

The little wireless patrol passed out into the night, its labors ended. Now that the excitement was past, the boys realized how tired and sleepy they were. As they crossed the Bay to their temporary home on Staten Island, they had their last view of the harbor. Now it was almost silent. Only a few boats were ploughing through its waters. The great office-buildings were dark. The fiery lights of the city were extinguished. But bright above the Bay flamed the torch of Liberty. There, in that flickering light, was symbolized the thing that millions of men were giving their lives to protect—the greatest heritage of the ages. And as the boys from Central City looked at the symbolic illumination, their hearts beat exultantly and their eyes grew dim with joy at the thought that they, too, had been able, through months of self-denial and rigid self-discipline, to prepare themselves for the task that was now so happily ended.

Choose from Thousands of 1stWorldLibrary Classics By

A. M. Barnard
Ada Leverson
Adolphus William Ward
Aesop
Agatha Christie
Alexander Aaronsohn
Alexander Kielland
Alexandre Dumas
Alfred Gatty
Alfred Ollivant
Alice Duer Miller
Alice Turner Curtis
Alice Dunbar
Allen Chapman
Alleyne Ireland
Ambrose Bierce
Amelia E. Barr
Amory H. Bradford
Andrew Lang
Andrew McFarland Davis
Andy Adams
Angela Brazil
Anna Alice Chapin
Anna Sewell
Annie Besant
Annie Hamilton Donnell
Annie Payson Call
Annie Roe Carr
Annonaymous
Anton Chekhov
Archibald Lee Fletcher
Arnold Bennett
Arthur C. Benson
Arthur Conan Doyle
Arthur M. Winfield
Arthur Ransome
Arthur Schnitzler
Arthur Train
Atticus
B.H. Baden-Powell
B. M. Bower
B. C. Chatterjee
Baroness Emmuska Orczy
Baroness Orczy
Basil King
Bayard Taylor
Ben Macomber
Bertha Muzzy Bower
Bjornstjerne Bjornson

Booth Tarkington
Boyd Cable
Bram Stoker
C. Collodi
C. E. Orr
C. M. Ingleby
Carolyn Wells
Catherine Parr Traill
Charles A. Eastman
Charles Amory Beach
Charles Dickens
Charles Dudley Warner
Charles Farrar Browne
Charles Ives
Charles Kingsley
Charles Klein
Charles Hanson Towne
Charles Lathrop Pack
Charles Romyn Dake
Charles Whibley
Charles Willing Beale
Charlotte M. Braeme
Charlotte M. Yonge
Charlotte Perkins Stetson
Clair W. Hayes
Clarence Day Jr.
Clarence E. Mulford
Clemence Housman
Confucius
Coningsby Dawson
Cornelis DeWitt Wilcox
Cyril Burleigh
D. H. Lawrence
Daniel Defoe
David Garnett
Dinah Craik
Don Carlos Janes
Donald Keyhoe
Dorothy Kilner
Dougan Clark
Douglas Fairbanks
E. Nesbit
E. P. Roe
E. Phillips Oppenheim
E. S. Brooks
Earl Barnes
Edgar Rice Burroughs
Edith Van Dyne
Edith Wharton

Edward Everett Hale
Edward J. O'Biren
Edward S. Ellis
Edwin L. Arnold
Eleanor Atkins
Eleanor Hallowell Abbott
Eliot Gregory
Elizabeth Gaskell
Elizabeth McCracken
Elizabeth Von Arnim
Ellem Key
Emerson Hough
Emilie F. Carlen
Emily Bronte
Emily Dickinson
Enid Bagnold
Enilor Macartney Lane
Erasmus W. Jones
Ernie Howard Pie
Ethel May Dell
Ethel Turner
Ethel Watts Mumford
Eugene Sue
Eugenie Foa
Eugene Wood
Eustace Hale Ball
Evelyn Everett-green
Everard Cotes
F. H. Cheley
F. J. Cross
F. Marion Crawford
Fannie E. Newberry
Federick Austin Ogg
Ferdinand Ossendowski
Fergus Hume
Florence A. Kilpatrick
Fremont B. Deering
Francis Bacon
Francis Darwin
Frances Hodgson Burnett
Frances Parkinson Keyes
Frank Gee Patchin
Frank Harris
Frank Jewett Mather
Frank L. Packard
Frank V. Webster
Frederic Stewart Isham
Frederick Trevor Hill
Frederick Winslow Taylor

Friedrich Kerst
Friedrich Nietzsche
Fyodor Dostoyevsky
G.A. Henty
G.K. Chesterton
Gabrielle E. Jackson
Garrett P. Serviss
Gaston Leroux
George A. Warren
George Ade
Geroge Bernard Shaw
George Cary Eggleston
George Durston
George Ebers
George Eliot
George Gissing
George MacDonald
George Meredith
George Orwell
George Sylvester Viereck
George Tucker
George W. Cable
George Wharton James
Gertrude Atherton
Gordon Casserly
Grace E. King
Grace Gallatin
Grace Greenwood
Grant Allen
Guillermo A. Sherwell
Gulielma Zollinger
Gustav Flaubert
H. A. Cody
H. B. Irving
H. C. Bailey
H. G. Wells
H. H. Munro
H. Irving Hancock
H. R. Naylor
H. Rider Haggard
H. W. C. Davis
Haldeman Julius
Hall Caine
Hamilton Wright Mabie
Hans Christian Andersen
Harold Avery
Harold McGrath
Harriet Beecher Stowe
Harry Castlemon
Harry Coghill
Harry Houidini

Hayden Carruth
Helent Hunt Jackson
Helen Nicolay
Hendrik Conscience
Hendy David Thoreau
Henri Barbusse
Henrik Ibsen
Henry Adams
Henry Ford
Henry Frost
Henry James
Henry Jones Ford
Henry Seton Merriman
Henry W Longfellow
Herbert A. Giles
Herbert Carter
Herbert N. Casson
Herman Hesse
Hildegard G. Frey
Homer
Honore De Balzac
Horace B. Day
Horace Walpole
Horatio Alger Jr.
Howard Pyle
Howard R. Garis
Hugh Lofting
Hugh Walpole
Humphry Ward
Ian Maclaren
Inez Haynes Gillmore
Irving Bacheller
Isabel Cecilia Williams
Isabel Hornibrook
Israel Abrahams
Ivan Turgenev
J. G.Austin
J. Henri Fabre
J. M. Barrie
J. M. Walsh
J. Macdonald Oxley
J. R. Miller
J. S. Fletcher
J. S. Knowles
J. Storer Clouston
J. W. Duffield
Jack London
Jacob Abbott
James Allen
James Andrews
James Baldwin

James Branch Cabell
James DeMille
James Joyce
James Lane Allen
James Lane Allen
James Oliver Curwood
James Oppenheim
James Otis
James R. Driscoll
Jane Abbott
Jane Austen
Jane L. Stewart
Janet Aldridge
Jens Peter Jacobsen
Jerome K. Jerome
Jessie Graham Flower
John Buchan
John Burroughs
John Cournos
John F. Kennedy
John Gay
John Glasworthy
John Habberton
John Joy Bell
John Kendrick Bangs
John Milton
John Philip Sousa
John Taintor Foote
Jonas Lauritz Idemil Lie
Jonathan Swift
Joseph A. Altsheler
Joseph Carey
Joseph Conrad
Joseph E. Badger Jr
Joseph Hergesheimer
Joseph Jacobs
Jules Vernes
Julian Hawthrone
Julie A Lippmann
Justin Huntly McCarthy
Kakuzo Okakura
Karle Wilson Baker
Kate Chopin
Kenneth Grahame
Kenneth McGaffey
Kate Langley Bosher
Kate Langley Bosher
Katherine Cecil Thurston
Katherine Stokes
L. A. Abbot
L. T. Meade

L. Frank Baum
Latta Griswold
Laura Dent Crane
Laura Lee Hope
Laurence Housman
Lawrence Beasley
Leo Tolstoy
Leonid Andreyev
Lewis Carroll
Lewis Sperry Chafer
Lilian Bell
Lloyd Osbournc
Louis Hughes
Louis Joseph Vance
Louis Tracy
Louisa May Alcott
Lucy Fitch Perkins
Lucy Maud Montgomery
Luther Benson
Lydia Miller Middleton
Lyndon Orr
M. Corvus
M. H. Adams
Margaret E. Sangster
Margret Howth
Margaret Vandercook
Margaret W. Hungerford
Margret Penrose
Maria Edgeworth
Maria Thompson Daviess
Mariano Azuela
Marion Polk Angellotti
Mark Overton
Mark Twain
Mary Austin
Mary Catherine Crowley
Mary Cole
Mary Hastings Bradley
Mary Roberts Rinehart
Mary Rowlandson
M. Wollstonecraft Shelley
Maud Lindsay
Max Beerbohm
Myra Kelly
Nathaniel Hawthrone
Nicolo Machiavelli
O. F. Walton
Oscar Wilde
Owen Johnson
P.G. Wodehouse
Paul and Mabel Thorne

Paul G. Tomlinson
Paul Severing
Percy Brebner
Percy Keese Fitzhugh
Peter B. Kyne
Plato
Quincy Allen
R. Derby Holmes
R. L. Stevenson
R. S. Ball
Rabindranath Tagore
Rahul Alvares
Ralph Bonehill
Ralph Henry Barbour
Ralph Victor
Ralph Waldo Emmerson
Rene Descartes
Ray Cummings
Rex Beach
Rex E. Beach
Richard Harding Davis
Richard Jefferies
Richard Le Gallienne
Robert Barr
Robert Frost
Robert Gordon Anderson
Robert L. Drake
Robert Lansing
Robert Lynd
Robert Michael Ballantyne
Robert W. Chambers
Rosa Nouchette Carey
Rudyard Kipling
Saint Augustine
Samuel B. Allison
Samuel Hopkins Adams
Sarah Bernhardt
Sarah C. Hallowell
Selma Lagerlof
Sherwood Anderson
Sigmund Freud
Standish O'Grady
Stanley Weyman
Stella Benson
Stella M. Francis
Stephen Crane
Stewart Edward White
Stijn Streuvels
Swami Abhedananda
Swami Parmananda
T. S. Ackland

T. S. Arthur
The Princess Der Ling
Thomas A. Janvier
Thomas A Kempis
Thomas Anderton
Thomas Bailey Aldrich
Thomas Bulfinch
Thomas De Quincey
Thomas Dixon
Thomas H. Huxley
Thomas Hardy
Thomas More
Thornton W. Burgess
U. S. Grant
Upton Sinclair
Valentine Williams
Various Authors
Vaughan Kester
Victor Appleton
Victor G. Durham
Victoria Cross
Virginia Woolf
Wadsworth Camp
Walter Camp
Walter Scott
Washington Irving
Wilbur Lawton
Wilkie Collins
Willa Cather
Willard F. Baker
William Dean Howells
William le Queux
W. Makepeace Thackeray
William W. Walter
William Shakespeare
Winston Churchill
Yei Theodora Ozaki
Yogi Ramacharaka
Young E. Allison
Zane Grey

www.ingramcontent.com/pod-product-compliance
Lightning Source LLC
Chambersburg PA
CBHW030321180626
46810CB00003B/1182